GRACE IS YOUR STRENGTH

Book Five

Francois Renault

Ideal Publishing
LightPublishing@aol.com

New York, New York
United States of America

First English Edition
F.J. Reynolds©2012

Library of Congress Card Number:
2012909678
International Standard Book Number:
978-0-9621682-9-1

Book Five of
Reflective Insights

DEDICATION

To the unified consciousness of humanity.

OTHER BOOKS
By FRANCOIS RENAULT

Reflective Insights - Introduction
Perfection Is A Process - Book One
Know Your Psyche - Book Two
Your Essence is Magnetic - Book Three
Balance is Your Foundation - Book Four
Picture It Perfect - Book Six
The World is Your Mirror - Book Seven

CONTENTS

12

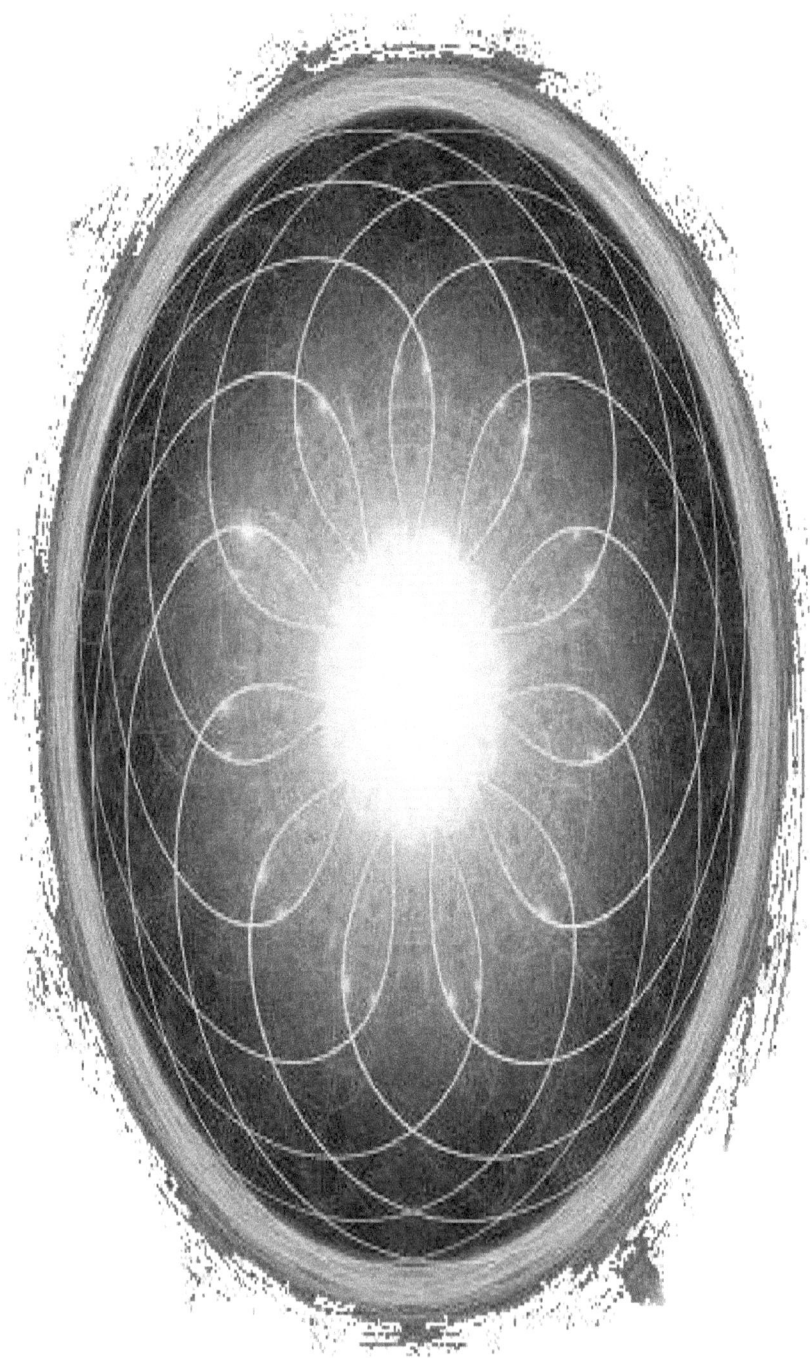

INTRODUCTION

THERE'S A LIGHT

The central message of this book is that each and every one of us can awaken from delusions of negativity, transforming ourselves and our world into a higher frequency of consciousness. The reader is encouraged to thoroughly scrutinize and rethink his or her concept of grace. In our ego-based world, many empowering concepts have been degraded and relegated to the fringes of reality — and this is very much the case for grace. An attempt is therefore made to clarify, rationalize and streamline this most important concept, which may be the ultimate key to humanity's success.

The power of grace has been one of the best kept secrets. This is partly due to leadership being afraid of empowering the masses with truth. Secondly, it is due to self-doubt within the masses. Furthermore, many individuals are leery of concepts that are difficult to analyze, for the ego is weary of spiritual insights. The bottom line is that human society has been founded on concepts of legalism and logic, because the ego is most comfortable with those systems.

Although its potential is amazingly powerful, grace has mostly been ignored by humanity. As a source of self-empowerment, it has been little understood. Yet it has been sorely needed in a world gone savage with competition and judgement. Just observe how most individuals treat each other during everyday living. For the most part, the ego has mostly judged grace to be impractical. Instead, it has focused its efforts on controlling others through legalism.

In some respects, grace has remained a relatively new concept — and yet it is actually a very ancient one, for it is a force that has been around since the beginning of creation. Due to its importance to human development, it is urgent that the concept be revealed for its intrinsic value.

Grace is a force that is both timeless as well as pragmatic, a power that can renew the mind as well as the heart. This understanding is especially urgent in today's chaotic, aggressive world, where the majority of the population live with hardened attitudes and hearts as cold as ice. It has been a world based on the harsh reality of judgement, where individuals are determined to be either worthy of respect or are treated as replaceable parts.

"Grace Is Your Strength" is not simply a book on surviving the rat race but on thriving and moving into a higher consciousness. It is hoped this book will help the reader make sense of the competitive, judgmental reality in which most of us live. Perhaps the philosophy shared within these pages will be found useful towards practical living. Considering the massive amounts of knowledge now available to us, it is unfortunate how little of it is useful for everyday living.

The approach taken is that of "humanistic philosophy," but a spiritual one with the potential to raise our consciousness. There is a vast difference between spirituality and religion. In fact, they are essentially polar opposites: whereas spirituality is about enlightening and empowering individuals, religion is about controlling and directing the masses. This is why some individuals have been turned off by the message of grace — because it has been clothed in religious apparel. It has been erroneously perceived as religious manipulation and therefore as an impractical doctrine left to the naive. Thus one problem with grace has been its misrepresentation, the manner in which its essence has been muddled with religious jargon.

Yet it is not really a concept about religion but about the human condition. Therefore, it is important that the religious as well as non-religious be awakened to the empowering aspects of grace, for it is a practical principle pertinent to everyone.

It is preferable to remove the concept of grace from a religious structure for several reasons. First, a religious presentation discourages universal acceptance. Second, we should respect differences in cultures. Third, the initiative to accept grace must come from personal choice rather than from external extortion. Each and every individual must experience his or her own spiritual introspection, for each of us has an individual point of reference. Therefore, each of us integrates grace in a unique manner. The revelations we eventually accept are unique to our individual level of understanding; we are empowered in ways pertinent to our personal needs. While the ego may resist enlightening ideas, our Higher Self will persistently cheer us forward with endless patience.

Grace as a practical philosophy covers many aspects of living. It is not only about finding one's purpose in Life; it is also about maintaining a balanced perspective on Life, as well as developing a sense of graciousness. When we cultivate grace within our lives, it softens the harshness of the world. It is a tool that helps us take control of our lives — especially where no control seems possible.

Yes, "the good news" is that there is a more enlightened way of coping with Life than what we have been led to believe. Grace entails a philosophical approach that is beyond judgement and fear, leading to a deeper and higher level of happiness. It is the key to a higher quality of life — one that empowers humanity as the divine beings we truly are.

Throughout history, messages of enlightenment have been attacked with deliberate force, until their light has been rendered seemingly impractical. This is how "amazing grace" became boring grace. In its place, the human ego established a harsh world based on legalism and rules for "proper behavior." Thus, in their coarsened hearts, many have found it difficult to open their hearts to the power of grace. The irony is that only an open heart will allow its expression.

The ego has a natural aversion to spiritual advice, preferring hard logic and cynicism to lofty insights. Such an attitude is an obstacle to real advancement: an ego which mocks spiritual concepts as impractical will be more comfortable with a philosophy based on competition and judgement. In reality, our present world is based on deceit and manipulation. On the other hand, grace develops a strong foundation based on idealism and honesty. Therefore, the ego needs to understand the practicality of grace in improving the human condition.

Let's look at what grace is not: (1) It is not an emotional state. Rather, it is a flow of openness. (2) Neither does it equate with expressive love, although the two concepts certainly overlap. A balanced life requires small doses of negativity intermingled with positivity. Although the power of grace does not necessarily erase negative expression, it does promote equilibrium within the full experience. And (3) it is not about performing acts of mercy or forgiveness, for grace perceives everything to be as it should be. **In one word, grace is *blessing***!

While no one is an expert on grace, we all have a Higher Self that promotes it. The objective is to present grace in a manner that can be accepted by the ego, regardless of its religious or cultural viewpoint. The presentation is written in a manner that hopefully will pierce through coarsened attitudes, so that the ego has a chance to appreciate grace from a logical point of view. Then, and only then, it might be willing to adopt grace as a worthy concept. Only then can a true partnership develop between ego and Higher Self.

Although grace is a divine concept streaming from

the higher realms of Life, the ego only understands its value through hard logic. Because the concept can be intimidating, only honest reflection can show the ego how grace can empower the human condition. Only then can its power lend itself to self-forgiveness and introspection.

Although the ego can be quite judgmental, it nevertheless hopes to be embraced unconditionally. We all want to be accepted the way we are; we want to be free to express our individuality. That is where grace comes in: it shines support on everyone, good or bad, without judgement. Yet it does not demand power or energy, for it comes to us free of charge, regardless of whether we deserve it or not!

Sometimes we may get tired of the bitterness, chaos and coldness predominant throughout the world. Sometimes we may feel ready to release the negativity in our lives. And sometimes we might feel ready to reclaim our innate divinity, to unify our ego with our Higher Self. The power of grace offers us these things, thereby allowing us to reach our full potential.

The power of grace is not really about forgiveness or any other active expression. It is a matter of respect and receptivity. It is about allowing expression and appreciating the worthiness of each and every individual, so that they can develop their lives as their Higher Selves see fit. It is about encouraging a flexible, enlightened mind-set, with the conviction that all individuals are important to our personal success. And as an added benefit, the process of acceptance eventually facilitates an increase in personal frequency.

References for this book are derived from a wide variety of sources, including psychology, physics, metaphysics, religion and intuition. One very important reference describes grace as *equative in nature*. In other words, grace can be described as a powerful equation, one that can be applied to our own personal human equation. The logic is as follows: because all things in Life are based on mathematical equations, then it follows that grace must also have a mathematical expression. Whether we speak of a molecule, force, rock or living entity, each and every thing is based on an equation. And as an equation, grace is a powerful principle that can assist us in reaching and maintaining the highest quality of life possible.

Grace will also be described as "common nirvana," for a state of grace is essentially of the same quality as a state of nirvana. Generally speaking, nirvana is "a profound peace of mind acquired by liberation from suffering." It is the enlightened state that spiritual gurus of the East aspire to. But for everyday practical living, a common form of nirvana is required — this is grace.

Of course, some cynics dismiss grace as a concept left to the naive. In their skepticism, they might suggest that since grace cannot be studied in the laboratory, it cannot have tangible, predictable effects. But on the contrary, it is a force with powerful effects! Everyday, in many ways, its power is experienced and validated on a personal level by countless people. In fact, it is the greatest gift that Life offers us — a simple means for integrating beauty, joy and respect within our lives. It frees us from the burdens of guilt and resentment, for it is a *spiritual nova* that overcomes darkness of any kind.

Ultimately it is more pragmatic if we can move beyond debating the merits of grace and simply implement it in our lives — enjoying its rich treasures of empowerment. *All we have to do is open up our hearts and claim this gift.* With technology moving fast forward, we need to equally fast forward our consciousness. However, by no means do we have to be saints; we need only do our best. For many, it will take years to fully switch gears in their life philosophy. But as the years go by, we will become ever more proficient in understanding the principles that move Life. The grace force will be our guide through an amazing transformation, which will complement other self-improvement techniques we may wish to practice as well.

We will learn to dissolve dramas of sin and karma, because power trips based on these only serve to diminish our character. Unfortunately, humanity has been obsessed with its own imperfections. But our Higher Selves encourage a much grander basis for living: offering us enlightenment based on grace & nirvana. All we need to do is open up our hearts!

Because Earth is destined to be transformed into a planet of enlightenment, humanity needs to awaken to spiritual insights. Such an awakening on a massive scale will be a sea change, shifting humanity into a higher level of consciousness; it will appear as if we became a new species. Our higher consciousness will then help us expand into realms never before thought possible. Thus empowered, we will finally find our rightful place in the scheme of things — as co-creators with Life.

CHAPTER ONE

A FREQUENCY OF BRILLIANCE

It is a fact that humans need the love of others to not only survive but to thrive as well. For instance, orphanages throughout the world have learned that babies must be picked up, rocked and touched on a regular basis. Otherwise, they develop severe emotional handicaps, or they fail to survive at all. Thus there is no doubt that love is essential for human development.

An interesting aspect of love is that we can love others without liking them. For example, there is the religious angle of "loving the sinner but not the sin." However, this is simply an attempt to promote *conditional* love by separating the sinner from the sin. This approach would never work with grace, because — by its very virtue — the true magnificence of grace never lends itself to such corruption. Divine grace can *never* be diminished into "conditional grace." No such thing can be! *Divine grace always refers to unconditional acceptance — and much more!*

Although grace does not equate with love, it is inclusive of it and then some. Grace encourages the expression of love, while *beholding* respect of all things. And whereas love expressively binds, grace promotes freedom and appreciation without restrictions. Thus grace is ultimately about freedom, an **allowance** for all things to express themselves as they are meant to be.

While love is an expression, grace is simply acceptance. Where love is an action, grace is a passive allowance. And whereas love is an emotion, grace is simply a *supportive* force. And lastly, while love is personal, grace can be personal as well much more — for it is extraordinarily universal and eternal. Grace does not require active expression; it is always there, simply waiting to be accepted. It is absolutely free, never requiring penance from anyone. Otherwise, a need for atonement would imply that grace is conditional on our behavior. And it is most definitely not!

Interestingly, forgiveness is not necessarily part of the grace equation, for such action is never required on its behalf. With grace, it is understood that there is *nothing* to forgive, because there is nothing to condemn. There is nothing to control; thus there is no power struggle to even acknowledge! It is important to understand that divine grace is *beyond* petty human dramas of manipulation. It is, in fact, a spectacular energetic equation based on divine essence. While love is said to be the Golden Rule, grace is the **Divine Code**. Not only must we learn to treat (love) others as we would have them treat us, but we must also learn to go beyond that — respecting everyone and everything as divine aspects of Life. This means embracing the understanding that everyone and everything is an important part of the big picture. Essentially, grace teaches us to respect all expressions of Life. We love because we *will* it; but we embrace grace because we *respect* the divinity of Life.

Contrary to much misunderstanding, integrating grace within our lives does not mean that we must remain in a state of love 100% of the time. It does not mean rejecting emotions of anger or disappointment, for they are all part of the human experience. While Life is composed of polarities (of opposites), grace insists that we not divide it into extremes of good and bad. It insists that we not label "badness" as either sinful or even unimportant. That is why the ego tends to rebel against the concept of divine grace — because it is more comfortable judging everything.

Whether we *feel deserving* of grace is completely beside the point, for it is outside of its scope — never requiring that we earn it. There are no restrictions. There are no general requirements. And there are no time limitations. Not only is grace without judgement, it is without rationalization. It is without boundaries and without expectations. All incidents — past, present, future — are held without judgement. Within the realm of grace, our behavior is neither condoned nor condemned. Grace exists as a gift free to all, without exception.

Unfortunately, much of humanity has mostly hidden within the darkness of fear and judgement. This has been of the ego's choosing. On the other hand, our Higher Selves exist within the perpetual blessing of divine grace.

So, beyond acceptance, what is grace? In simple terms, it is divinity, devotion, joy, patience, contentment, thankfulness and graciousness. These are characteristics which tend to be contrary to the ego's nature — which is more comfortable with competition and judgement. In fact, the ego often finds the idea of grace somewhat irritating and confusing, because its view of the world has been polar opposite of this ideal. The ego understands very well the need to survive in a world full of criticism, but it finds it difficult to comprehend the practicality of divine reverence for Life.

The roots of the word "grace" go back to the Greek "charis," which means "I am glad, I rejoice." So the original meaning refers to joy and happiness. It is unfortunate that many individuals probably think in religious terms when they hear the word grace. This occurs because concepts tend to get corrupted as time passes; their meanings tend to deteriorate. Thus today, most individuals understand grace to be no more than being grateful to others, "saying grace" before meals or simply showing mercy. Often, people have difficulty moving beyond concepts of judgement and legalism into a grander concept of "reverence for all."

Furthermore, grace is not so much an achievement but a realization. The difference between achievement and realization is somewhat similar to that between legalism versus spirituality. While grace is divine in origin, in our physical reality it manifests as **spiritual humanism** — encompassing attributes of compassion, respect and blessing. *It is a philosophy of personal empowerment based on a sense of veneration for all.*

While the expression of love can take many forms, grace is essentially the same within all its reflective states. Nevertheless, the underlying foundation of grace is about living in joyful reverence for Life. Although grace is reflected in many facets of Life — from expressions of forgiveness to elegance — it is still basically the expression of acceptance. Regardless of its specific reflection, grace transcends ordinary life, encouraging us to move forward, higher and wider, as we come to understand the divine nature of Life.

The original definition of grace as joy and beauty is still core and integral to its power. In fact, embracing grace within our lives implies a quiet quest for joy, a clearing away of the darkness that accumulates through years of negative drama. In reality, grace is the natural state of humanity, even though most of us have forgotten this blessed state. It is otherwise known as Xanadu! While personal happiness can refer to a subjective sense of well being, real bliss refers to a state of harmony in the presence of grace.

As we analyze the principle of grace, we will come to realize that the logic behind it is quite simple. This is because its essence does not originate from the ego, which is a creature of logic. Rather, it is a "frequency of brilliance" originating in the soul, where there is no need to prove anything through logic or rationality. As the natural state of Life, it is simply self evident to the Higher Self.

Looking at grace from an artistic point of view, we see that it is not about fixing others but about respecting their individual circumstances. It is about acknowledging that everything and everyone belongs within the eternal spectrum of Life. *The movement of grace is like that of a flowing river: it is powerful yet embraces the changes it encounters; it flows with strength yet it saturates its surroundings with its essence.* A philosophy based on grace is about making conscious choices based on appreciation, beauty and wholeness. It is about encouraging others with their own success, while seeking to learn from them as well. It is about embracing an attitude of "so be it." It is about surrendering the right to get even. (Yet, needless to say, it does not mean losing the ability for self-defense.)

A grace-based philosophy encourages the destruction of score cards, for it is not about repaying others according to their merits — but according to their needs. In fact, the word *deserve* never applies. It is about understanding that compassion is at the core of Life. Divine grace — which manifests as common nirvana — is a state of appreciation for the inter-connectedness of all things and people, for it is the glue that holds everything together. Grace is peace, as nirvana is peace. For it is only when we transcend our emotional afflictions that we are able to achieve the peace that is so elusive to most of us.

While knowledge simply puffs up the ego, grace strengthens the self from within. It softens the heart and promotes a gentle joy, where neither darkness or hatred can remain. An embrace of grace leads us into greater visions where it is understood that all "wrongness" can be absolved. It is knowing that every single experience is valuable because it leads us into perfection. That is, all experiences can lead the *ego* towards perfection, for the Higher Self already exists in divine perfection.

But grace is not about positive thinking, although it

is one of the results. And it is not about memorizing formulas or laws but simply about expressing our true divine nature. It is about releasing negative perspectives within a framework of *allowance*. The power of grace works on two levels: limiting the destructive effects of judgement while expressing our divine essence. And since the Higher Self is already divine by nature, it does not feel the need to prove anything. The ego, on the other hand, finds grace to be an alien concept. Therefore, for the ego, it is a learned phenomenon.

The ego initially scoffs at the idea of grace not only because it is described in such sweeping terms but also because it is not based on a "give and take" approach. It perceives grace as something for the morally lazy; it prefers the comfort of legalism and judgement — which provide a concrete sense of *control* over the environment. The ego is especially uncomfortable with the manner in which grace bypasses legalistic systems with apparent loopholes. It is also uncomfortable with its power to break chains of drama, since drama is a means by which the ego manipulates others. The ego prefers to hold humanity in moralistic bondage because it is an experience it can relate to.

In fact, the principle of grace may seem threatening to the ego, until it is ready to embrace its empowering nature. When the ego consciousness finally accepts grace, it does so in small steps: understanding it as joy, approval and support. These are the simple, concrete ways in which the earthly ego is able to gradually understand a divine concept that appears alien to it.

But grace is much more than that! It is a real, distinct energy, just as electro-magnetism is an unseen but real force. A physicist will confirm that Life is a composite of frequencies, and every frequency has its own specific, unique expression. In terms of physics, a frequency is a force with recurrent, cyclic expressions. And as a frequency, grace is so brilliant, so perfect, so exquisite that it overcomes and erases inharmonious frequencies. In visual terms, it is a geometric fractal of tremendous beauty and complexity. (A fractal is a geometric shape that can be split into parts, each of which is a reduced copy of the whole.) Someday, this fractal will be calculated mathematically, but for now it can be understood to be the most eloquent of all expressions. As an equation, it makes little sense to the ego, but it does not need to understand it in mathematical terms. It need only develop the conviction that grace is the grandest, most lyrical frequency that exists anywhere in the universe.

As the most perfect of all frequencies, divine grace pulses with expressions of "yes" to everything — to Life, joy, experience and individuality. Within the human arena, it expresses as altruism and nurturing. It is a power of pure *acceptance* and harmony, breaking egotistical reactions of blame and judgement. It pierces darkness as an ethereal light of divine splendor, a euphony of pure joy and appreciation. It is a "song of songs," resonating as a healing force that dissolves all sense of isolation.

CHAPTER TWO

LEGAL TO CONTROL

The way of the world has been a somber one, for it is founded on rigidity, fear and judgement. Not surprisingly, researchers consistently find that over 90% of humanity is dysfunctional. Many individuals lack vibrancy, substance and balance. In fact, they tend to feel that their lives are "dirty." And instead of learning to cleanse themselves in spiritual terms, they tend to succumb to ever heavier frequencies, choosing lives based on contention. This sad state of affairs is due to ignorance in regards to the true nature of Life. Nevertheless, it is possible for people to change their approach. When they become aware of their potential, they can shift their consciousness into a higher state.

Generally speaking, most people tend to develop a

shell around their persona, choosing to stay in ruts of drama. Of course, this is not a conscious choice; but this is what they feel most comfortable with. Many downtrodden individuals choose the way of darkness because it is what they are familiar with. Rather than embrace a philosophy based on light, they scorn it as impractical and something strange.

What most confounds the ego is the manner in which grace encourages us to appreciate the importance of *all* human beings — even the bad ones! The ego, being of judgmental character, finds this concept both irritating and unacceptable. In fact, the power of grace agitates those who are most comfortable with dark principles. In a world that has fallen from grace, where intolerance is tolerated, judgmental attitudes go unjudged and narrow-mindedness is defended as "logic," we are all declared to be deserving of punishment. For example, religious leaders often rail against "immoral lifestyles" as the work of demons. But it never occurs to them that their own ungracious attitude is motivated by demons as well! Evil is known to spread through societies like an airborne disease. One religious egomaniac can easily infect a whole society — because "misery loves company."

Gifted psychics sometimes describe a condition which plagues a majority of humanity, where negative energy attaches itself to the bodies of individuals. These forms of negativity include frequencies of shame, resentment, revenge, cynicism and apathy. In appearance they look like dark balls of "curled-in" energy. They have even been described as being "ghoulish" in character. Because they crave energy, they induce us to express drama, over and over again, ad nauseam. Through such emotional expressions, they gain strength. At times they multiply by splitting and jumping onto others who may be in proximity. But this scary condition does have a cure! Like a vaccine, the power of grace rids us of these parasites; it also prevents psychological degradation.

Many individuals continually suffer from emotional poisons that saturate the world. Cycles of abuse tend to perpetuate themselves, until they eventually suffocate any sense of spirituality within its victims. These dense energies make it difficult for us to view Life in the clearest form possible. In fact, it can lead to a type of insanity — one promoting hatred and violence. This process is self-evident; simply observing the daily news confirms this fact.

It is true that societies use legalized violence to control illegal violence. Misinformation is spread as well, in order to control the masses. Sometimes the lies may sound logical, and laws based on them may even appear necessary.

44

This is because much of the misinformation is deliberately backwards (or opposite) from the truth. *In this manner, we are surrounded and corralled by powers which promote confusion.* Simply put, the darkness of dogma and propaganda are enforced to keep the masses under control for the convenience of the elite. It is certainly not for the benefit of the common citizen! Nevertheless, proponents of control techniques usually don't know any better — for they are also simply pawns to their own dark masters.

Living by spiritual truths has been difficult, because we have been trained to be spiritually blind. Yet, there have been a few rare individuals who have persevered, ultimately "seeing the light." It has been a matter of unraveling misinformation and appealing to their Higher Selves. Such an endeavor is pursued by brave souls who know better; they know that scorn and judgement are not the highest standards to live by. Thus it should be understood that lies and fear are the basis for dark control, but freedom, tolerance and respect are celebrations of Life. We can remain part of the ignorance, or we can wake up to the deeper truths of Life!

Needless to say, we all have darkness and light within us. From the beginning of time, there has been a constant give and take between our earthly egos and our divine selves. This struggle was envisioned as a normal, healthy rhythm — a means to develop and propel an ever higher consciousness. Unfortunately, as a species, not only have we degraded into a shadow of our real selves but we have grown mostly comfortable with the status quo. Our egos have increasingly sunk to ever deeper darkness, creating hellish situations throughout the world. We need only read history books to confirm this observation.

The problems that we see within human society result from our ego-based persona. Deep inside most individuals churn feelings of disdain for humanity as a whole. Of course, this does not mean that humanity is evil by nature, for all of Life is composed of polar opposites. The real problem has been that we have looked to the ego for sole guidance, and the ego only understands aggressiveness, survival of the fittest and judgement. But since our Higher Selves are also an integral part of our makeup, there is always hope for improving the human condition.

Certainly, our history is proof that an ego-based world is not a model of enlightenment. This is not a matter of criticizing the ego, for the ego has its place and role in the development of humanity. Its specialty is the earthly realm; yet it sorely needs guidance from the Higher Self. It is a matter of shifting our consciousness from one based on the ego to one based on the Superconscious. As the necessity for such a shift in consciousness is recognized, our mental gears will be re-directed.

One of the ego's solutions to humanity's problems has been religion. Religious leaders have consistently claimed that no one can be truly happy, fulfilled or "saved" without belonging to their religious institution. In reality, religion is simply the ego's means to controlling the masses; it is the ego's interpretation of reality. When the masses are controlled, the elite feel they are in charge, safe and secure. While free individuals may appear as "wild cards," institutions define rules for acceptable behavior. Within such structures, the masses are more predictable and easily directed.

Religious leaders have spent enormous amounts of time debating concepts of "truth." And of course, every religion defiantly insists that its version of the truth is the only real one. According to various religious dictations, one can only gain approval from the Creator by following prescribed patterns of behavior and worship. The claim is that we will be blessed over those of different religions. Their myopic views are truly pathetic to those who know better and refuse to be boxed in by religious doctrine.

For the most part, religion has not been a real solution to humanity's problems. If it were, we would now be living in a near paradise! Again, we need only open a history book and view the evidence. Unfortunately, religion has mostly served to divide and crush the human spirit. It is as if religious leaders fear that some might find real spirituality elsewhere.

The problem is that religious dogma is based on egotistical values, a means to harness the masses for the good of the elite. *Religious institutions are run by legalistic principles — a form of ungrace which demands that we earn our way to approval.* To the ego-oriented, this system appears perfectly logical. However, it has been a very limiting arena for the development of human consciousness. It has discouraged individuals from seeking higher guidance from within. Sadly, to even suggest that the Creator can be reached by the common soul is considered blasphemous by many religious leaders. Yet, what is blasphemous about creations looking for their Creator? The real blasphemy is lying to humanity, teaching that we are not worthy as divine souls, that the only salvation lies in following strict rules of behavior. Those who step outside of boxed religion clearly see that religious dogma is a dead-end path for human evolution. On the other hand, when we strive for spirituality, we learn that grace is not only enlightening but also empowering. Therefore, it is to our benefit to move away from legalistic dogma and into studying divine insights.

Looking at history, it is clear that *ego-based legalism* has been a toxin passed from generation to generation. It has stripped religion of a spiritual nature, removing divinity from the human equation. And THAT has indeed been a crime! For example, the most severe law within legalistic religion requires "an eye for an eye." In the minds of those in power, legalism has been a most logical, necessary means to maintaining balance of justice. And of course, religious leadership has been delighted that the masses have agreed to live under dictatorial forms of religion. Yet, in a world where unspeakable atrocities have been committed in the name of religion, it should be obvious that boxing God into religion has been impractical, unfair and certainly a failure.

Perhaps the ego has made a sincere effort to address karmic/sinful issues. But its solutions have been developed from the lowest denominator, which have not fully acknowledged higher levels of thought. In being rigid with their absolute adherence to tradition and judgement, legalists have demonstrated the opposite of grace. While they may appear clean and pure on the outside, trying to impress others with their religiosity, legalists tend to be quite corrupt inside. The religious system is a failure in another regard: its subjects are *forced* into "goodness."

Legalism always leads to extremism because it demands strict forms of behavior. Its power has grown exponentially, constantly moving to extinguish joy and real hope, for these are threats to religious leadership. Under legalistic systems, we are made afraid to make mistakes that might violate any number of laws. As a result, our main concern becomes how best to avoid condemnation, criticism or punishment. Rather, as divine souls, we should be dancing to the rhythms of Life. We do not have to PROVE our worthiness to anyone. There is nothing to prove! Rather, the most important point in living is to celebrate the variety of Life!

Throughout history, grace has mostly been ignored, sometimes mocked, and other times even assaulted. Some cynics have disdained the concept of grace as unrealistic and too idealistic, something left to the naive. These attacks have left the masses confused, causing them to view the principle as impractical and surreal. If humanity has continually fallen further out of grace, it is because religious leaders have failed us. They have mostly rejected divine grace because they have been unable to utilize it for controlling their followers.

When we give our personal power to religious leaders, we conspire with them to destroy the divinity within humanity. By rejecting personal responsibility, we give up our rights as well. In that respect, we can not blame others for our sad state of affairs. While we learn to recognize legalists as grace killers, we must also learn to respect ourselves as worthy of its benefits. At the same time, it is important that we do not become consumed with fighting legalism, for it is really an endless struggle of egos.

While legalism is based on keeping score cards, grace completely erases them, encouraging us to revere the endless variety of Life. According to legalism, people suffer because they deserve it, because they are punished for their karmic dues or sinful attributes. They teach that we must "prove ourselves" through some form of sacrifice, which may include physical denial or punishment.

The ego has had ample time to prove its methods are real solutions for "salvation." Unfortunately, its crude philosophy has been based on the principle of retribution, which only removes us further from our natural state of grace. In fact, to even suggest that we have a higher divine nature is often considered blasphemous and a mockery.

In fairness, many religions do incorporate intrinsic truths within their doctrines. And grace has certainly been one of these valuable truths! Other religions teach the value of reaching a state of nirvana, which is a state of grace. However, it is important to understand that the principle of grace is not necessarily a religious concept; it cannot be monopolized by any specific group or denomination. Rather, it is *a principle, power and equation* that exists independently of any established religion. It is an energy that continues outside of any human institution. Religions, being creations of the ego, would love to utilize grace to control humanity, but they have failed to find the means to do so. Thus, grace has been mostly neglected and relegated to the "useless" category.

Of course, religion has been — and will continue to be — important to millions of people. They cling to their religion, hoping that it will enrich their lives with goodness and shield them from evil. Unfortunately, they have been oblivious to the fact that the opposite has often been true: that they have been lead astray from true spirituality. The negative consequences of belonging to a religious organization have often been more severe than devout followers are willing to admit. For instance, many psycho-social problems have been created by religious dogma. If anyone wishes to deny this, they only need to think about all the wars and hatred that have been waged in the name of God.

The term "legalism" refers to a system of forcing morality on others through ever-stricter laws. These laws could include prohibitions on smoking, drinking, dancing, dating, sex and even pets! Thus a legalistic religion is one replete with rules, regulations and guidelines for acceptable behavior. The problem is that religious legalism encourages hypocrisy and mental sickness. Furthermore, it encourages confusion, egotism, resentment and bigotry, while it also discourages spiritual enlightenment. A great spiritual leader once said that if everyone followed the "eye for an eye" principle of justice, eventually the whole world would go blind!

The more ego-based our personality is, the more we feel comfortable with a legalistic approach. On the other hand, a wider view of Life suggests a higher consciousness. This contrast can be perceived as philosophies of "might makes right" versus "right makes might." In other words, while the ego sympathizes with the power of "might," the Higher Self understands that "right" is ultimately the more powerful of the two. When right is on our side, we have the upper hand.

Wise individuals have always emphasized the importance of respecting individual paths to perfection; the hardest thing is trying to be what others demand us to be. We must be true to ourselves by following our bliss, wherever the heart may lead. Imposing institutionalized ideals is another form of legalism. It strips respect from the human equation. By imposing their own ideals, religious leaders are able to separate the "worthy" from the "unworthy." As grace killers, they are then able to manipulate their followers with guilt trips.

Perhaps legalism began as a sincere effort to address karma or sin. However, whatever the original motive, legalism has accumulated ever more power through the centuries, until unspeakable atrocities have been committed in its name. In adhering to dogmatic "absolute truth," legalists have demonstrated that an ego-based philosophy is not the answer to humanity's problems.

While legalists often appear squeaky clean on the outside, their inner corruption eventually leads to self loathing. This is because the ego tends to swing from one extreme attitude to another. Sometimes it tries to compensate for a low self esteem by puffing itself up with false pride; at other times it feels that only self mutilation can "save" it from damnation. In fact, legalism actually exasperates and compounds the ego's frailty by forbidding "mistakes." Legalism becomes so self consuming that its followers are not even aware that they have become spiritually enslaved.

Humanity has reached a crossroads where many individuals are now open to universal principles. With a leap of faith, the ego can learn to live by grace, making it a real, integral aspect of its life. It is, in fact, a principle prevalent throughout the universe. It is found in the natural world, where plants and animals "simply are" ; they do not have to prove their worth in the scheme of things.

Sitting within a realm of divine grace, our Higher Self radiates eternal patience and compassion. It is incapable of judgement, condemnation or disdain for the ego. It simply awaits a world where legalistic reproachment is replaced with respect, with people encouraged to sing their own tune and everyone willingly moving to the rhythm of grace.

CHAPTER THREE

THE VALUE OF BEING

The value of the ego is in its capacity to help us navigate through the material world. But because it can be defensive in nature, it often distorts the true nature of reality. It has an independence of its own, having the power to react to circumstances, either negatively or positively. In other words, it can be destructive; or it can be constructive. By this means, it has the power to adjust our personal frequency. But it can choose to switch gears into higher or lower expressions at any time. Thus the importance of the ego is not only for self-preservation; its navigational capabilities are valued as well.

Because it is composed of a "monkey essence," the ego mind often jumps from issue to issue in an erratic manner. And unfortunately, it easily develops many destructive, reactive habits. For self-preservation, it tends to create a psychological shell for blocking out truths it may find threatening. Yet in reality, the ego is quite fragile. It easily succumbs to feelings of insecurity, especially feeling threatened by the unknown. Part of the reason it tends to get defensive is because it has limited resources. Thus it tends to reject anything that does not fit within its boxed view of reality, because it is not sure how to handle unknown situations. And when the world fails to respond to its needs, it naturally reacts aggressively. So when we base our personality on the ego, we tend to project frequencies of fear and insecurity into the world as well.

The ego consciousness has a limited view of the universe, one focused on limitations. And as long as we remain ego-oriented, we fail to see the bigger picture. Yet in reality, everything is interconnected and unlimited. The ego, being of limited nature, finds it difficult to accept this understanding. And until it accepts the true value of Life, the egotistical mind will reject spiritual insights. In fact, it gets aggravated at the very thought that there are values greater than its own biological needs. Thus it attempts to trap us in power struggles; the objective is to distract us from other topics and back to the importance of self.

Of course, the ego is important to our personal well-being, for it serves us well in its number one purpose: survival. It has enough consciousness to learn from its mistakes, and it has the power to switch mental gears at any time. It is also able to loosen its rigid views of Life, once it learns to relax. With training, patience and a leap of faith, the "monkey mind" is then able to assume its greatest role — that of partnering with the Higher Self.

The ego feels vulnerable because it knows that its essence is impermanent and that its powers are limited. Because it can feel insignificant within the bigger picture of Life, it struggles for self validation, constantly seeking a sense of control. It struggles for a sense of self importance and normalcy. The problem is that normality is an illusion; no one is really normal. In fact, it is a concept invented by the ego.

In a higher sense, one can describe the ego as *"perfect imperfection"*; while the Higher Self can be referred to as *"divine perfection."* The first term may seem like a self contradiction — and it is; but Life is full of apparent contradictions. While the ego has the capacity to learn basic intrinsic truths, it can only do so in a limited manner. On the other hand, when we base our personality on our Higher Self, we come to understand that we are already perfect souls. Yet, for physical existence, there is no way around needing the ego. Furthermore, physical experiences provide us with challenges that can expand our understanding of Life.

So-called karma and sin are created over time by judgements expressed by the ego. The simple mind criticizes everything, fights concepts of all-inclusiveness, and encourages us to divide the world into strict groupings of good and bad. And even when it is able to embrace higher ideals, it promotes itself as morally superior for having done so. Unfortunately, it has a habit of continually falling back into a sense of self importance. While the

Divine Self judges nothing and values all experiences, the simple mind is in constant discord with such divine values. Nevertheless, without such contradiction, without resistance, we would have nothing to work with. There would be no polarity to help us grow in ever-widening understanding. Thus, the ego is valued by the Higher Self for its "perfect imperfection" — *because it offers material to work with.*

Through honesty and perseverance, the ego can change; it can learn to partner with the Higher Self; and it can adjust personal equations to include divine concepts. While our "monkey consciousness" has dominion over the material world, our divine consciousness rules the ultimate reality of Life. Thus in partnership with the Higher Self, the ego's power can increase exponentially. But the ego must take a leap of faith, choosing partnership, for it alone can make that decision.

Needless to say, there are many obstructions to this ego-Higher Self partnership. In order to remove such hindrances, we must modify the ego's outlook on life. But this can only be done through total honesty. For example, until we are able to embrace universal insights, we remain hostages to the ego's limitations and misgivings. Many individuals get stuck in negative expressions of reactiveness, ignorance and improper use of willpower — which develop into cycles of drama. This can happen when we misplace our confidence in the ego's values. While true confidence is based on inner knowing from our Higher Selves, egotistical confidence is based on a flawed foundation of self delusion. This occurs when the ego fears the unknown and feels compelled to pull our consciousness back in bondage. Yet in reality, as divine entities, we are naturally fearless, compassionate souls. Thus, while fear can grow out of the ego, compassion springs eternally from the Divine Self.

Few individuals are able to fully integrate their lower and higher selves in a balanced, *graceful* partnership. But when they do, they can appear super human to the average person, because they manifest powerful, almost miraculous abilities. These are the souls that history has held up as truly "enlightened" and as children of God.

If grace empowers us, why is the ego inclined to resist it? Why is the ego more comfortable with incessant worrying, power struggles and obsessions? It's because higher ideals appear quite alien to the ego's animalistic nature. The ego's defensive attitude developed as a result of the "survival of the fittest" environment prevalent in the world. As it has struggled to survive in a competitive world, it has come to believe that every strike against it requires an equally aggressive reaction. It learns to believe in a power based on repaying evil with evil, the principle of "an eye for an eye." Yet, as it has struggled to evolve in its own way, it has mistakenly focused on a sense of contamination through karma and sin. Thus it has become highly judgmental of itself and others. And *the more it embraces judgement, the more it contracts in consciousness*. The result is a psychological foundation built on false confidence.

False premises lead the ego to confuse "perfectionism" for perfection. In reality, the two concepts are diametrically opposing ideas! Such misunderstandings have led many towards arrogance and revulsion — expressions that poison the consciousness. Historically, such egotistical expressions have led to downgrading of humanity's frequencies. Spiritual development never results *directly* from ego density. On the contrary, without spiritual guidance, the ego remains ingrained within a narrow, stubborn mentality — doubting and mocking ideas that it cannot possibly comprehend fully. As the ego experiences painful repercussions, it doesn't tend to loosen up. Rather, it tends to contract further, intensifying its desire to tightly control its immediate environment. Whereas, the ego should ideally take responsibility for its experiences, it prefers to redirect the blame elsewhere.

Due to our dualistic psyches, we are challenged with a chasm between animal consciousness versus divine consciousness. For those individuals who have been unable to assimilate the mental duality, the result has been confusion and narrow-mindedness. On the other hand, an expansive consciousness manifests within those able to meet the challenge. Negative expressions stemming from the ego can be transformed into learning experiences. They don't have to be destructive; they can propel us into higher levels of understanding. We can transform self crucification into equanimity. We can transition from "living by demerit" into "living by grace."

In terms of developing our consciousness, the foremost value of our ego is in its power to react to surrounding circumstances. It can choose to be negative; or it can choose to be positive. It can choose to be destructive; or it can choose to be constructive. Its spiritual value is in being able to shift our identity to the Higher Self, where the dichotomy is appreciated for all its possibilities. For this shift to occur, the ego must be willing to embrace the widest view possible, perceiving the interconnectedness of all things. Certainly, it is not about disavowing the ego but of appreciating it as the earthly half of our complete essence.

Understanding that the Higher Self appreciates the ego as "perfect imperfection" diminishes the ego's sense of insecurity and insignificance. It narrows the chasm between our higher and lower psyches. While the ego tends to perceive ugliness and danger everywhere, the Superconscious appreciates beauty and opportunity in every situation. To the Higher Self, Life is about choices, experiences and the challenge of rising to an ever higher consciousness. In lieu of remaining mired in fear and shame, we are encouraged to strive for higher ideals. *And grace is certainly the only tool that can sustain us in this endeavor.*

While the ego's inclination is to show kindness only to those who show kindness to it, grace encourages us to radiate respect and understanding to all. Interestingly, the opposite of grace is not hatred but indifference. History is full of examples of people standing by while innocents are deprived of justice or even their lives. This happens when the ego becomes the dominant consciousness within us, moving us to believe that the only important factor is our own survival. Yet, at the same time, it is dangerous to judge others, whether they be villains or victims. Because our personal world materializes from the unique energy equations we express, we co-create the realities we experience. So, if we focus our consciousness on the belief that humanity is inherently evil, the world responds by manifesting that experience in our lives. On the other hand, if we embrace the power of grace, we enforce concepts of hope and trust within our lives. Based on this understanding, the Higher Self never judges any of our behavior as good or bad; this is an understanding the ego consciousness can learn to embrace as well.

Too often, we feel overwhelmed by stressful situations, unable to maintain a sense of control. Yet we must remind ourselves that *we always have choices* in our lives. In particular, we always have the power of choice: we can choose between feelings of victimization or empowerment. We must never forget that we always have the power to color our lives with either cynicism or grace. That choice is always before us. This means we are not the victims that we sometimes perceive ourselves to be. Too often, the ego focuses on the narrow view that the world is a battlefield, an arena of constant conflict between good and evil forces. That is the ego's emphasis, for it evolved in an environment of "survival of the fittest." However, the Higher Self — the Superconscious — originates in the highest of dimensions where everything is understood to be part of divine order. *Everything* has its place in the grand scheme of things.

Nevertheless, it is important to acknowledge that the ego's outlook is not completely incorrect. In reality, we do have polarities to contend with. That is, we do have to choose where to focus our consciousness, for there are naturally occurring conflicts in the world. But we do not need to emphasize the conflict; we can underline the unity and cooperation of Life. Because the objects of our attention are drawn into our lives, we need to focus on the interconnectedness of all things. Grace transcends the principle of polarities — the schisms, conflicts and drama in our lives — smoothing out the bumps and grinds which the ego has come to expect. The ego's hardened attitude, with its ungracious experiences, can be softened and redirected through this divine power.

Eventually, the philosophy of "an eye for an eye"

will be superseded by divine grace, because vindictiveness, resentment and revenge will never bring us the lasting happiness that we all crave. The bruised ego only knows to counter attack and inflate its sense of self-importance. It justifies its demands of others, while constantly pointing out its own gestures of reconciliation. It convinces itself that it has every right to defend its physical and emotional well-being — *and it does have that right.* However, its habitual "mental accounting" — the constant adding up of good and bad behavior of others — is without end. Everywhere the ego looks, it finds bitterness; often, it feels caught between polar concepts of forgiveness and justice. While the Higher Self advises unconditional understanding, the lower self screams for justice and payback.

The immorality that the lower mind perceives throughout the world often motivates it to atone for its sins or karmic dues. Its primitive attitude often leads the ego to various self punishing activities. However, guilt trips are never productive avenues. Nothing truly positive results from self mutilating experiences. Endless rules meant to regulate "goodness" within the ego are just that: endless. For the most part, religious dogma to which many individuals enslave themselves does not improve the soul. Religious dogmas are simply psychological chains meant to restrict our thoughts and movement. They do not really help us move upwards into higher realms of understanding. Self torture and religious regulations are not the way to divine perfection.

The truth is, divine understanding is totally opposite to what the ego tends to believe. Yet when the ego can relax and open up to the Divine Self, the result is an amazing sense of freedom and illumination. It leads to a type of consciousness that has been labeled common nirvana. It is "common" because it stays with us throughout daily living. While spiritual nirvana is frequently associated with enlightened gurus, common nirvana is for common living — it is about living regular lives within the sphere of grace. It moves us away from cycles of drama, tuning our consciousness into higher frequencies of joy, understanding and appreciation. It quickens our personal frequency so that the grinding that we normally feel becomes a vibrant dance of ecstasy. And THAT is the beautiful alternative to the religious dogma that many attempt to force onto others.

We can begin the healing process at any time by refusing to play the role of victim. For that matter, we must simultaneously stop condemning the validity of personal experiences. We must realize that all experiences are meant to serve a higher purpose. What is done is done; experiences should be appreciated for their value in educating us, and then we must be able to move forward. We have the power to switch gears; we have the power to appreciate old experiences as well as forthcoming ones. Integrating our dualistic consciousness helps us realize that all experiences are within our control, even if only in the manner in which we react.

Eternally patient, the Higher Self has watched as the ego alternately plays the role of victim or aggressor. In the most loving way possible, it persistently reminds its lower half that there are things in Life grander than mundane dramas. The Higher Self only knows to forgive the "monkey mind" for being less than ideal, because the ego expresses itself as best it knows. At first, the ego may rationalize that grace is impractical: After all, if everyone were forgiven for their constant imperfections, then no one would be compelled to strive for betterment. But the truth is quite the opposite. *It is judgement that discourages people from striving for perfection* — a perfection where only our personal best is required. But the ego must learn to listen to its higher half; and then it must be willing to choose accordingly. Initially, it only understands survival, yet it eventually learns that there is more to Life than that. Its sphere of understanding can expand to include a thriving life style based on the highest ideals possible.

Too often, we become obsessed with the flaws we perceive around us. Thus we attempt to control every detail of our lives. However, such "flaws" are meant to teach us about different angles to Life; they are not meant to serve as psychological restrictions. While criticism is the foundation upon which legalism is based, the only way to reach our full potential is by expressing ourselves in the most enlightened manner possible.

If we are to shift our lives from one based on egotistical expressions to one of divine ideals, then we must understand ourselves. We must know that the four major factors of human expression are: 1) beliefs, 2) emotions, 3) attitudes and 4) habits. These factors are important to us, as we come to understand how and why we react to specific circumstances. When any of these factors are out of balance, we fall back to our egos by default. The plight of human potential has been stifled by the disequilibrium of these factors in negative mode. The key is to embrace them in positive mode, for they are what make us human. The choice is always before us: Do we wish to base our lives on a monkey consciousness that perceives Life with pettiness? Or do we wish to express ourselves through a higher consciousness that judges only the real issues?

The problem with many egos is that they develop a self-righteous attitude, which prevents them from recognizing their own flaws; yet they choose to focus on the imperfections in others. Unfortunately, few individuals truly aspire to live by the highest divine ideals. Of those that do, most are eventually degraded by a society based on legalism. It is not that humanity is evil or even stupid by any means; it is that most individuals base their lives on the ego, which is not specialized for ideal living.

Regardless of our flaws and failed experiences, we CAN shift gears from that of simple survival to one of "reaching for the stars." Because our attitudes are mirrored back to us, it gives us the feedback we need to manipulate our environment. We can shine the light of grace on our personal darkness, for dark things only grow in the absence of light. We do not need to retreat into the coldness of pure logic, for there it reflects very little light.

It seems that the older we get, the more brittle our egos become. Such brittleness is a sign of weakness, of becoming more fragile. As we get older, we should be getting more flexible. We should be getting wiser, learning to live in the most eloquent manner possible.

Ironically, the key to spirituality is not denial of the ego but acknowledging its importance and striking a balance. For instance, when we feel materially lacking, our egos become obsessed with physical survival. And when we become unbalanced in such manner, it proves difficult to strive for spiritual ideals. Being completely balanced means being able to embrace divine ideals while remaining firmly grounded in the physical world. Of course, we all know through personal experience that this is not an easy accomplishment. That is why few are holistically balanced: We can easily find wealthy individuals; and we can find spiritual gurus; but very rarely is an individual truly both. When they are, they are usually morally corrupt "pretenders of truth."

An excellent motto is: "Grow to live, and live to grow." It reminds us that our path should be perpetually based on inspiration. If our lives become stagnant, then we must change our path. There should be no hesitation in changing gears. By learning from our mistakes, we empower ourselves, for that is the purpose of Life. Thus it is impossible to play the Game of Life without making "mistakes." *When we vow to learn from each and every one of our experiences, we are reflecting our lives with perfection.* It is sound logic: If we are learning from our "mistakes," then they are really "learning experiences." Of course, the ego fights this simple logic — even though it is a creature of logic. It prefers to judge and reprimand. Here is where the power of grace can help. It encourages the ego to be flexible with its philosophy, as it learns to accept "failures" as lessons in Life.

When we live within the light of grace, we are free to move forward to ever higher heights. It gradually becomes easier to accept experiences with minimal judgement. While a brittle ego tells us that forgiving others is condoning their actions, grace reminds us that everyone has the right to be themselves. When we feel emotionally bruised, our pain becomes tightly wound within us, continually drawing more energy of the same frequency. This process can cause us to feel victimized. However, such an attitude is an indication of resisting responsibility; and if we do, it is equal to giving our power away.

Of course, there are aggressors as well as victims in the Game of Life. It is common sense. But a distinction is made between "habitual" victimization and "random" victimization. The latter, where one is attacked "randomly," can and does happen to anyone. The key is resisting entanglement in cycles of victimization.

The true meaning of "turning the other cheek" means resisting aggression as to not empower it. It is certainly not about taking a submissive, victimized role — for it takes much more courage and self control to resist stooping to a lower level. Of course, our egos tell us otherwise: that we must not be cowards, that we must protect ourselves at all costs. However, it is understood that the ego will stubbornly hold on to its values, because it reacts according to what it understands.

Besides judgement, the ego also believes in limitation as a primary fact of Life. Because Nature is perceived to thrive on competition, it is expected that there will be winners and losers. The ego considers this fact to be core and integral to surviving in the three-dimensional world. Admittedly, Life can be a struggle. Yet the Superconscious views Life as a roller coaster that should be enjoyed: Life is an arena of unlimited opportunity! The two views are simply mirror images of each other. Is one perspective truer than the other? Of course not; both are equally correct, even if they appear contradictory — because Life is full of apparent contradictions.

For most of humanity, there are many deterrents to living by higher ideals. Even in a modern society where knowledge is widespread, many individuals feel lost and disempowered. While religious dogma offers solutions, it is usually of a conditional sort. Thus living by grace is the only practical alternative.

There is an ancient saying, "If you live by the sword, you die by the sword." Likewise, if we live by the principle of score keeping, we will forever remain stuck in cycles of drama. On the other hand, if we live by grace, our lives will unfold with grace. The truth is, no one can beat a system of score keeping, for it perpetually self-sustains.

Eventually, we all trip. But imbalances are simply mirror images of balance. We are meant to learn from them: disequilibrium is not punishment. Imbalances manifest as sin or karma, but they should be understood as "wake-up calls," so that we can learn from them and move forward. It is expected that there will be a give and take between polarities within the arena of Life, for polarities are simply part of continuums. Thus we are forced to choose between understanding the bigger picture or falling to victimhood.

Personal experience is an arena often explosive with drama. If we don't know better, our personal relationships eventually translate into power struggles. This happens when at least one individual refuses to expand his or her consciousness, so that the relationship stagnates into drama. Because the ego is defensive by nature, it finds it easier to blame others when things go wrong. On the other hand, striving for higher ideals implies that we are willing to accept responsibility for our personal happiness.

80

We do not have to keep score; nor do we have to judge others for being less than perfect. If drama predominates in a relationship, partners are free to walk away. There is no shame in ending self-destructive circumstances. Nor do we have to be righteous, which is the ego's insistence on always being right. When we truly know that we are right, we are not afraid to keep it to ourselves; it is a reflection of spiritual maturity.

We must never give up on ourselves; and we must never give up on hope. When we come to believe in our full potential, there is no end to our success. Because Life is about making choices, we can choose to do the right thing — being true to our selves.

CHAPTER FOUR

COMMON NIRVANA

The state of maintaining graciousness throughout daily living is known as "common nirvana." This is different from the state of nirvana that spiritual gurus strive for. In Eastern philosophy, nirvana is a frame of consciousness in which we are freed from suffering, while simultaneously finding union with the Source of Life. The word "nirvana" literally means "blowing out" — as in blowing out the fires of negativity, hatred, greed and delusion.

Common nirvana is about developing psychological resources that help us express our consciousness in the most creative, balanced manner possible. This process is integral to the integration of our consciousness, one in which we unify our lower and higher psyches. The force that propels us forward on this path is hope, for without this powerful concept, we would lack the initiative to seek a higher and wider understanding of Life.

Although the word "hope" may be one of the most over used words, it is perhaps the most powerful concept in our vocabulary. Because without hope, we would be incapable of striving for better conditions. It inspires us to improve ourselves as well as our societies. It gives us reason to strive for more than mere existence — to thrive. It instills us with purpose: The purpose of Life is to live a life with purpose; and that purpose is reaching for divine perfection.

However, the difference between "perfectionism" and "perfection" must be understood, for they are actually polar opposites. While perfectionism refers to the ego's external attempt to feel good about itself, perfection is the actual integration of **knowing** the importance of our role in Life. And while the ego-based perfectionist habitually criticizes flaws, true perfection means striving to appreciate the eloquence of **all** things in Life. It is about understanding that "mistakes" are simply spiritual insights; they are stepping stones on our path to perfection.

Obviously, there is a major distinction between the ego's concept of perfection and the Higher Self's understanding, which perceives everything and everyone as already being perfect. The Higher Self knows that everything is **perfectly geared** to move us towards ever greater consciousness. This includes the ego: It is appreciated for being "imperfect," for it is **perfectly** designed to entice our consciousness with challenge, thus moving us forward on the path of perfection. Without the ego, there would be no room for improvement, for we would simply exist in a perpetual state of divine perfection, where there are no problems or disequilibrium; nothing would agitate things into a state of creativity. Instead, the ego is programmed to shake things up. It does this with stubbornness, arrogance, selfishness, narrow-mindedness and judgement — characteristics we normally view as negative! But in the great divine plan, negativity plays a proper, constructive role as well — motivating us to strive for ever higher and wider insights.

It is simply part of the bigger picture in which the principle of polarity plays its creative role.

While the ego is persistent in its discriminatory approach to Life, the Superconscious is equally persistent in reminding us that we are already perfect — if only the ego would accept this truth! Due to its design, the ego understands perfection to be a process; while our Higher Selves already exist in perpetual divine perfection. This is why our two psyches — ego and Superconscious — are perfectly set up to complement each other: It is the perfect scenario for movement of energy, resulting in a wide variety of learning experiences.

In general, the ego tends to resist the concept of divinity, because it is focused on the harsh reality of survival. Material survival is its number one objective. As a result, it looks for vulnerabilities within the material world. Erroneously, it defines perfection as "never making mistakes." But the ego eventually stumbles upon a splendid insight: If we are willing to learn from our mistakes, then they are not mistakes at all! They are learning experiences! Simple logic clearly shows the ego that mistakes do not have to be mistakes. It is our choice whether to learn from our experiences or relegate them to the trash category.

For the Superconscious, "mistakes" are simply important factors in the grace equation. It understands that "errors" are essential for the learning process. <u>All</u> experiences can lead to perfection — it is up to us to define their worth! In the universal court of Life, divine grace declares us clear of sin and karma, for perfection is already inherent within the human experience. We need only embrace the understanding that learning from our mistakes transforms them into positive factors. There is no need to fear change, no need to resist new endeavors; we must simply learn how to move gracefully through "bad" experiences for the lessons they are.

The power of grace takes the edge off the ego's harsh attitude. It emphasizes the importance of accepting everything as part of the bigger picture, as part of the equation of "perfect imperfection." We are exactly the way we are meant to be in our present state of development. *When we live in grace, there is no need to prove our worth to anyone.* We simply live our individual perfection as best we can, without judgement or validation. We always appreciate our personal effort, no matter how far from target it may fall. Grace diminishes the ego's need for any kind of justification or absolution. We don't even have to justify our right to grace — it is simply part of the divine plan. We only have to embrace it, knowing that sin and karma do not have to be part of the human condition. When coming to this realization, we cease to see others as imperfect beings. Rather, we come to perceive them as the divine souls they are — souls seeking "enriching" experiences, for they are as children relishing adventure.

Through the ages, the ego has voluntarily imprisoned itself within a darkness of sin and karma, for it has firmly believed it deserves no better. However, humanity is now reaching a state of consciousness where it is ready to shift into higher gear. *Against the dark realm the ego has created, divine grace shines as the most brilliant of equations — like a diamond with endless beauty and sparkle.* Gently but firmly, its power pierces through the ego's darkness, its illumination dissolving cynicism and judgement.

Integrating the ego and Higher Self results in a startling metamorphosis. Yes, the ego is essential for physical survival; and it will remain an integral part of self identification. Yes, we will continue to incorporate degrees of judgement in daily living. But we will gradually integrate ourselves into a complete whole. We will learn to follow the "knowing" of being in the right place at the right time. Not only will we learn to follow our divine intuition, but our higher frequency will trigger powerful codes within our genetic structure. And as these codes reach full expression, they will open our consciousness to new abilities: "And you shall do even greater things!"

Thus embracing common nirvana in our lives leads to self empowerment. It encourages us to express our selves as victors rather than as victims of circumstances. Of course, the ego will continue to be itself — making judgements — for that is its intended nature. But in the process, it will also evolve to an elevated state, where it will be in a better capacity to learn about Life. As common nirvana moves us through new experiences, they will be of a more enjoyable nature, and karma/sin will manifest in milder forms.

Nevertheless, we must certainly not delude ourselves into thinking that grace will lead us to 100% happiness. Why not? Because Life implies *integrating* polarities within our experiences — not *eliminating* them. Furthermore, when we adapt to conditions, we gradually take them for granted. The process of adaptation tempers even the most powerful experiences, so that they eventually lose their sense of importance. Thus, as we advance in consciousness, we will come to understand that we cannot remain permanently "happy"; there is no such thing as a static situation in physical reality. Since "variety is the spice of life," the key to contentment is experiencing Life within a flow of yin and yang circumstances.

There is also the distinction between physical happiness and spiritual happiness; the latter stems from a sense of purpose. Common nirvana — as the highest form of happiness — is a matter of constantly balancing our negative and positive experiences. It is a matter of knowing that negative experiences enhance our positive ones. Thus continuous euphoria is not a practical objective, for pure happiness does not last perpetually. However, by integrating graciousness within our lives we are able to raise our "set point" for happiness. This means striving to appreciate present circumstances while simultaneously moving towards higher and wider ground. It means *appreciating* truth and beauty in everyday reality. While focusing on "ugliness" attracts more of the same, uncovering the beauty within our lives inspires us and conditions us to perceive even more joy.

Common nirvana is a personal pursuit, because it is defined by our own values. We decide how to enjoy our precious moments; we decide what objectives to pursue; we decide how to move forward. Thus according to our values, we project our consciousness into the world. It frees us from psychological prisons of our own making by "blowing out" negativity. And as we learn to appreciate ourselves, we learn to extend the same gratitude to others. Grace liberates and uplifts the heart; and so it uplifts the world.

Common nirvana is *not* about reaching the empty nature of reality. Rather, it is a continuous, daily uplifting of consciousness. It is the gradual development of a luminous consciousness that expands the ego's perceived boundaries of self. And as our sense of self expands, we are led to understand that all things are interrelated within the arena of Life.

The grace equation promotes a revolution of the heart, expanding it beyond the bondage of karma and sin. Rather than focusing on the imperfections of the ego, we are encouraged to embrace divine perfection. As the ego relaxes, it is able to relinquish its destructive nature and focus on its pro-creative abilities. The gift of grace sets us free, empowering us to say "no" to controlling dogma, "no" to mental slavery and "no" to victimhood.

When we integrate common nirvana within our lives, we are inspired to reach for ever higher ideals. We are encouraged to express our energy in the most constructive manner possible, to manifest our divine creativity in the world. And as our hearts continue to expand with graciousness, our understanding will expand as well. Our legacy as co-creators will shine through the brilliance of grace — resounding and illuminating our true divine origins throughout the universe.

94

CHAPTER FIVE

THE GIFT OF LIGHT

From our Superconscious' perspective, every aspect of Life has an important role to play. Nothing is considered wasted; nothing is devalued, for everything is simply a piece of the bigger puzzle. Thus integrating grace within our lives is about encouraging the ego to look beyond its pettiness and to think more within the bigger picture. It is about going *wider* as well as higher with our consciousness, so that we expand our perception of Life. The ego's potential can expand, so that it learns to appreciate its crucial role in our learning experiences.

Instead of resisting the Higher Self, the ego can choose to embrace it; it can learn to understand its "crazy" metaphysical ideas, for they do not have to be perceived as a threat to its survival. Our lower and higher psyches can become powerful allies: While the ego provides zest and challenging points, the Divine Self provides guidance and a supportive structure.

Yet the ego must still take a leap of faith. It must be willing to expand its consciousness, by thinking in wider as well as higher terms. Ordinarily, the ego tends to think hierarchically; while the Superconscious views things from a wide horizontal perspective. And although the ego is obsessed with its self-importance, the Superconscious appreciates the importance of everything, without rank. For this reason, the union of our lower and higher psyches is represented symbolically by the equilateral cross — the perfect union of vertical and horizontal consciousness.

Because the ego's approach to Life is vertical, it creates social structures that are controlled by the elite. This occurs within religious, political as well as economic institutions. It has been about separating humanity, between the worst and the best. Of course, this concept is a psychological trap, because "undesirables" have to exist at the bottom of hierarchical structures. This is a common manifestation within churches, where the "holy" preside over the "sinful" masses. And outcasts are relegated to the bottom, usually threatened with damnation of some kind. So hierarchical religions need sinners to function, so that the elite can maintain control from the top. Expressing religious structure in such a fashion is a corruption of what is perceived in the greater vision of Life. The various levels of life that one finds within Nature is not about separating the good from the bad. It is simply the manner in which life-forms naturally find their niche within their environment. No where in Nature does one find life defining itself superior to other life forms.

In the process of unifying our vertical and horizontal psyches, a wider perspective of Life becomes the norm. As it develops a partnership with the Superconscious, the ego learns to let go of its primal fears. It learns to respect rather than fear powers that manifest as a result of this union. Such supernormal abilities are understood to be powers of light. Certainly, when they are solely within the grasp of the ego, such powers can have devastating results. But a unification of our lower and higher psyches means that the Higher Self provides guidance, while the ego drives the expression.

As unification of our lower and higher minds develops, many pieces of the bigger puzzle fall into place, making progressively more sense to the ego consciousness. And as the ego modifies its thinking, the subconscious re-writes its mental software as well, providing a clearer and more expansive algorithm. In fact, in order for grace to manifest fully within our lives, the subconscious must be reprogrammed. Its mental software must be upgraded, and destructive loops must be erased, for they promote never-ending cycles of drama. As the ego's fortress gradually softens, negative programs are released and replaced with inspirational concepts. Initially, one may feel overwhelmed with the changing fluctuation, but a sense of equilibrium is eventually re-established. Since each personality is unique, so is the process of re-wiring the subconscious' programming.

Life at its most intrinsic level is about frequency. Our consciousness is a type of tuning fork that adjusts its resonance according to external frequencies. But it also works in a two-way process: Our consciousness is affected by its environment, but it also initiates its own frequencies. When the ego and Higher Self establish a common resonance, they radiate a most extraordinary frequency, thereby unfolding our true legacy as divine souls. Of course, it is not about developing a sense of superiority but of radiating a quiet "knowing." It is an understanding of the importance of all things and persons, and radiating this outwards in a steady flow.

Our three-dimensional world is one of constant highs and lows — a wild coaster ride of extreme falls and sharp turns. These extremes are especially common when our ego and Higher Self are at odds with each other. This causes hardship and confusion, as old doubts continually slip back into our consciousness. But such dark moments of self doubt can be a positive thing, if they trigger self analysis; they remind us of the immense power inherent within the ego-Superconscious partnership.

"God helps those who help themselves" refers to the importance of the ego taking the initiative, while allowing the Superconscious to fill in the details. If we attempt to force things into our lives, the result is a gross experience. On the other hand, when we allow our Divine Self into our personal equation, our lives are experienced as "going with the flow," a feeling that things are meant to be. In other words, we become part of solutions rather than adding to problems; we are able to "rise above the fray."

When we choose ego-based cynicism, we set ourselves up for personal failure. Yes, many individuals do become materially successful by forcing their consciousness in the world. In fact, it has been considered the norm. Yet once the game of wealth is won, many "successful" individuals hit a rock wall of discontent, where they sense spiritual emptiness. Sometimes the emptiness has a positive effect because it forces them to shift gears, so that they adopt new endeavors of higher caliber. They learn to re-direct their attention towards objectives of a higher nature.

From our Superconscious' perspective, Life is a playground where we can freely express our personal frequencies. It perceives an arena where we can dance to our own music, where problems are simply understood to be "wakeup calls." Thus it promotes the praising, uplifting and supporting of others; it certainly does not condone judging, controlling or demeaning others. The ego is inspired to ride turbulent experiences as a surfer rides a wave. And just as a surfer may occasionally fall, likewise we are expected to occasionally make "erroneous" decisions. Thus we are encouraged to yoke our ego's willpower with divine intuition, to balance them within an eloquent equation. Such an equation serves as a foundation for the highest, most successful reality possible. It is the key to creating experiences that encourage the child within us to fully express itself.

Intuitive messages are real, tangible frequencies that are meant to guide us through the turbulence of everyday living. Divine messages are certainly not reserved for the elite, for they are given to each and every soul, without rank or reservation. The Divine does not speak solely to the "worthy." Everyone is important within the wide expanse of Life. Nevertheless, inspiration is worthless if it lands on a sterile, cynical attitude. Seeds of inspiration must land on fertile ground, where the consciousness is receptive to higher endeavors. Skepticism feels like concrete to inspirational thoughts, insuring that they shrivel and die. Yet a receptive attitude is not enough. After inspiration must come aspiration — the willingness to act.

Within the realm of consciousness, what defines our worth is not where, when and how often we have erred — but how we rise from our troubles. It is not so important where we have been but the direction we choose to go, the objectives we choose to focus on. Thus we need to fall in love with ourselves — with our *whole* selves. We need to remain open to endless possibilities and wondrous events, for Life is full of surprises — beautiful ones! Learning flexibility means embracing "mistakes" as guideposts to an ever-wider "perfect imperfection." So-called sins and karmic debts are meant to be learning experiences — not prisons of self-pity and unworthiness, for they do not allow us to live at our highest potential. Life is about living as divinely and perfectly as possible, without fear and without forcing it. Our divinity awaits patiently, quietly coaxing our ego into appreciating "mistakes" as part of its personal equation, for it is the only way to express the perfection already inherent within us.

While the secret to spiritual success lies in unifying our Higher Self with our ego, we are also subject to **universal laws of Life**. They are meant to frame our reality as they guide us through everyday living. The seven main universal principles are listed below, but they are discussed further in Book 4. They are as follows:

EVOLUTION: Perfection is a process.

SELF-AWARENESS: Introspection leads to truth.

EQUALITY: All forms are equally appreciated.

BALANCE: Equilibrium is the natural state of all things.

LOVE: Loving others is blessing oneself.

RESPONSIBILITY: Accountability is self-empowering.

ONENESS: All are interconnected as one consciousness.

These laws apply to our consciousness and should not be confused with the seven *universal principles of creation.* (See Book 6.) Furthermore, above these tenets, grace shines the brightest because its purpose is to smooth out the bumps and grinds caused by "imperfections." As each of us moves towards our personal perfection, the path is paved by the grace we manifest within our lives. Otherwise, without grace, we remain stuck within ego-based realities — cycles of drama. Indeed, our highest state of expression is that of grace. While the ego is important to our physical survival, yet it is only interested in physical power and status. ***Thus it is important to expand our personal equation to include an ego/divinity essence: While the ego's imperfections are stepping stones towards perfection, grace sustains and balances.*** It is only when the ego becomes receptive to grace that it is able to fulfill it highest role within our lives.

While reverence is the way of the Superconscious, irreverence tends to be the ego's trip. Accepting the divinity of all things seems alien to the ego. Still, deep within all of us is a desire to connect with Life. Grace fulfills this purpose; it is the algorithm that shines where it is needed, smoothing out the bumps and grinds caused by the ego's agitations and rejections. It heals and balances where universal laws are pushed out of sync. Thus it is not a matter of being "saved" but of becoming synchronized with the whole of Life. It is not so much a matter of atoning for our sins or karma but of reaching a balanced state within the bigger arena of Life. Its valued wonder is that it has no requirements — for grace is a force that exists precisely for times of hardship, when we feel crippled with feelings of worthlessness and hopelessness. As an independent force, it is a melodic equation of equilibrium.

Yes, grace is many things! It is a multifaceted gem of energy; it is a code, an equation, an algorithm as well as a force of energy. In poetic terms, it is the cooling breeze of Life, forever flowing around us. When we tune ourselves to its frequency, we set our mental sails to it, floating off into beautiful horizons. By attuning to its power, our consciousness can shift into ever-higher degrees of understanding. On the other hand, if we embrace cynicism, we move contrary to the very nature of Life; we remain entangled within hells of our own making.

In simple terms, grace is "the other side of love." While love is a pro-active force of willpower, grace is a passive reverence emanating from our Higher Selves. As the highest frequency, grace smooths out conflicts that develop between other vibrations. Since everything is energy, human-made frequencies can clash, causing interferences of various proportions. This can happen when the ego rejects the importance of things in the greater flow of Life.

Someday, the mathematical equation of grace will be determined. But for now, it is only important to understand its psychological value, as represented here: *Grace = Compassion + Reverence + Inclusiveness.* As the highest force within Life, it sustains and nourishes everything, without exception. Its only requirement is receptiveness on behalf of its subjects.

When we look at atoms under a computerized microscope, we do not see things; we see only *energy* expressed as frequency. If *everything* is a frequency, then it follows that we are also frequencies; we are a conglomeration of frequencies. That is, each of us is composed of various frequencies, the totality of which is unique to each individual; we are energy with specific patterns.

To understand the bigger picture of Life, we must accept that everything has its own specific frequency signature. And as conscious entities, we have the power to manipulate the frequencies found within our environment — both in our immediate area as well as in unseen distances. In fact, we have always manipulated our environment according to the quality of our thoughts, because how we choose to react to our experiences affects our reality. It is important to always remember that **personal choice _is_ power;** and no one can take that from us.

As the most brilliant frequency in the universe,

grace is not owed to any one or any thing — it is free to any and to all! Everyone is deemed worthy and important to the stream of Life, but grace has to be chosen of our own free will. Regardless of our state of development or personal frequency, it is available to us only when we *choose* to receive it. While Nature is in a state of perpetual reception to grace, humans have to learn to accept it, because of our free will.

As the universal equalizer, grace is a frequency of the clearest light possible, its purpose being to clear away obstructions that jam communication between ego and Superconscious. Such hindrances block messages of empowerment, love and unity, forcing us to survive by our egotistical wits. On the other hand, clear channels of communication empower us to reach for the stars, whereby we fulfill our utmost potential.

As we clear away obstructive forces, our view of Life becomes ever brighter. We come to appreciate the value of divine insights. We come to realize that everyone is important to the overall success of the human race, that above all, respecting everything includes respecting ourselves. We learn that "imperfections" of the ego are simply challenges for the expression of grace. This insight is common sense to the Higher Self but it is an understanding that must be learned by the ego.

While the ego tends to perceive separation as the norm — for example, itself versus the world — the Superconscious understands that everything is really interconnected. In reality, there are no divisions except those projected by the ego. Thus the Higher Self continually impresses the importance of honoring the variety and connection of all things within the greater expression of Life.

Contrary to many dogmatic, religious views, accepting that we have a divine self is by no means blasphemous or egocentric. Rather, it is about realizing that we have a *responsibility* as co-creators with Life, that we are creative *movers* in the Game of Life. Embracing this insight is about reflecting maturity. If we reject our responsibility as co-creators, it is because we maintain an egocentric focus on reality. Because the ego has difficulty understanding a reality beyond separation, its biggest illusion is that we are simply animals with sophisticated brains. But it does have the capacity to stretch its consciousness to embrace ultimate truth: that we are a god consciousness embodied within biological machines.

Self-reflection is not simply self absorption. Rather, it is about waking up from the slumber in which humanity has been trapped for millennia. Dense frequencies have degraded us into the "walking wounded." However, the time has come for humanity to liberate itself from cycles of drama, which have only served to denigrate us and hold us hostage to pettiness. As we strive for common nirvana, unifying our split personalities in the process, we will truly come to appreciate our "perfect imperfection." We come to appreciate that there is no judgement regarding past transgressions; they can no longer hold us back. We are free to move forward in consciousness, embracing all our experiences for their spiritual worth.

Certainly, "perfection" can be described as a *state* of being perfect; but it also refers to the **process** of moving towards perfection. Striving for perfection means appreciating the sacredness of all things — especially ourselves! Regardless of our sins or karmic debt, we are no less sacred. On the contrary, those experiences exist to glorify us, to move us beyond a static existence. We were created to reach for the stars. And the time has arrived for humanity to claim its rightful role as co-creators, for we are not meant to be victims but *movers* of reality. As a young species, manifesting the power of grace will renew our hearts, so that once again, we will be rediscovering the magic of Life.

114

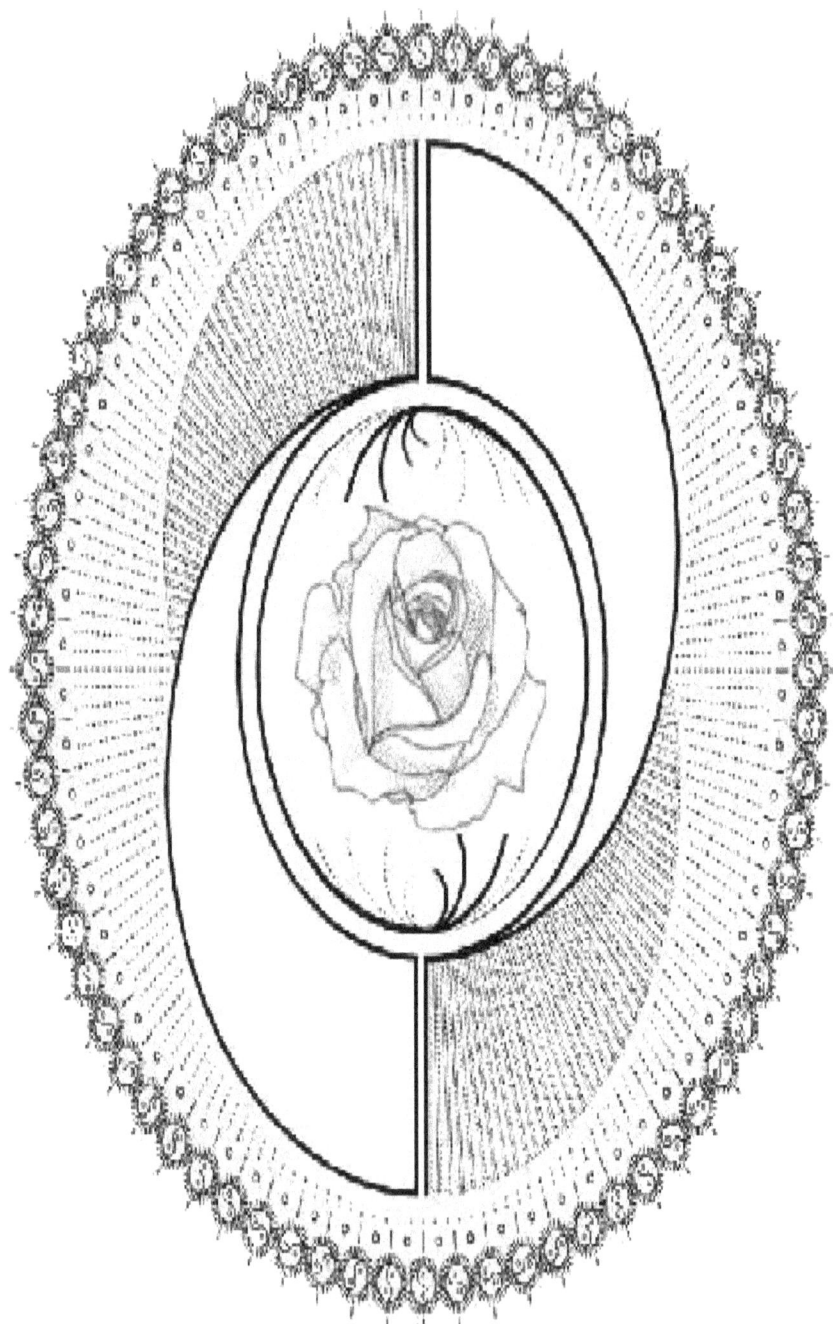

CHAPTER SIX

DEVOTION IN MOTION

Only through the heart can the ego fully understand the power of grace. Thus, in transforming our consciousness, the ego needs to move beyond personal "errors." First it must move to a higher state of mind, where dark experiences are transformed into spiritual adventures; this is a mental place where the ego's self-destructive tone transitions to self forgiveness. Then it must be willing to move even further to a state of grace.

Although grace and forgiveness are commonly thought to be the same thing, they are actually different expressions. Yes, grace and forgiveness are related, but they are also distinctly different from each other: While grace is an expression of our Higher Selves, forgiveness is the ego's best effort to emulate it. And while grace is above drama, forgiveness is the ego's response to emotional pain. Most importantly, forgiveness implies that there is something to *earn* back. Often, we nurture resentments, awaiting a plea for forgiveness from those who hurt us. In doing so, we enable others to draw us into cycles of drama. This is because the act of forgiveness is part of a back-and-forth dynamic involving actions and reactions; it is based on a foundation of conditions. It implies that *something* must be done to bring justice. And it demands that both "victim" and "aggressor" remember the offending incident.

Since divine grace originates in the highest realms, it moves above and beyond the ego's arguments. It denies the requirement for forgiveness of any kind, for any reason. And this is why the ego has difficulty with the concept — because it perceives every unjust act as requiring an equally forceful reaction, thereby leveling the playing field. But while forgiveness requires willful action, grace simply wipes the slate clean, without any expectations whatsoever — it sees nothing to forgive! Grace breaks the cycle of drama instantaneously! It demands nothing, expects nothing, forces nothing. It breaks cycles of resentment by simply erasing all debts, without reacting to anything. It simply embraces and blesses, regardless of the circumstances. It teaches that all of Life is divine, that everything has its importance in the bigger picture.

Of course, it is not suggested that forgiveness is unimportant in our lives. It is only emphasized that we understand two things: (1) forgiveness stems from the ego's basic need for give and take; and (2) the expression of grace originates from our Higher Selves, which simply offers unlimited understanding, without reaction. Having underscored these points, it is nevertheless normal that the ego desires acts of forgiveness. The individual who can forgive *completely* actually transmutes the act into something that approximates grace. When we genuinely forgive, the ego consciousness moves closer to divine consciousness. Thus, when we practice forgiveness in our lives, we should attempt to forgive without conditions. We forgive because we deserve inner peace, a life without baggage. Above all, we must forgive ourselves for being less than perfect, for the ego is as it is meant to be — "perfectly imperfect." In this capacity, it fulfills its true value to the Higher Self.

While forgiveness and resentment are polarities within cycles of drama, grace moves beyond the dynamism of polarity. It is about moving above taking sides, about perceiving blamelessness in all experiences. That is the true meaning of "turning the other cheek" — not reacting to blows, because reactions draw us into cycles of give and take. While forgiveness is an active and reactive principle, the power of grace simply instills *allowance* into the heart. Its power is passive in nature — but it is a very real power, nevertheless. Those who are unable to invite grace into their hearts are doomed to live by the ego's crude rule of an "eye for eye."

Actions for transformation. The simplest way to transform ourselves through grace is attitude. First, we must be willing to view ourselves with complete honesty. Initially, the process may be painful to the ego, for it is a very fragile, insecure creature. Contrary to the tough image it attempts to portray, it is actually quite brittle and easily shattered. It is quite relentless as well, constantly coercing our consciousness to focus on survival as its number one objective. On the other hand, it is not very good at moving beyond survival mode, to higher states of consciousness. Yet with patience and understanding, it *can* learn to surrender to the Higher Self. It can learn to sit back and enjoy the ride, while the Superconscious takes the steering wheel. Indeed, the ego and Higher Self are meant to be partners in the Game of Life, together moving into higher states of consciousness.

With the mentality of a restless monkey, the ego often jumps erratically from topic to topic. It is inclined to distract us from topics it considers surreal and impractical. Such subjects are deemed irrelevant to its search for comfort and power. Specifically, it tends to consider grace a worthless concept. Survival of the fittest is the name of its game. However, when the ego is able to grasp the practicality of grace, it can make a leap of faith. By applying the ego's own values of logic and rationality, it can be convinced that grace can improve quality of life. Its intransigence can be dismantled by dissolving its inclination towards cynical self-destructiveness.

Due to the ego's nature, it requires *physically expressive means* in order to integrate grace within its mind-set. It needs tangible activities — exercises based on logic and willpower which it can relate to, for these are factors predominant in its physical realm:

·**Intent.** This is the most direct way to reach common nirvana. When our specific intention for grace is focused and put into practice, we are training the ego to appreciate the variety of Life. As we gradually re-orient our views, we learn to express gratefulness in all circumstances — such as perceiving the silver linings in all experiences. As we gradually retrain the ego to appreciate each and every moment, we draw the frequency of grace into our lives. This is because frequencies of similar nature are drawn to each other. It is a basic law of energy.

Needless to say, it is difficult for many individuals to shift their attitude from legalism to altruism, which is an expression of grace. Nor is being cheerful all the time a realistic approach; the effort would eventually sink us into ever deeper levels of depression. What is proposed is that we embrace "mistakes" as valuable aspects of our lives, as learning experiences. Most of us tend to hate, deny or cringe in regards to our so-called mistakes. Often we hope that they do not follow us in our lives. This is where grace as a key fits perfectly: unlocking our ability to overcome sin or karma. The process of grace works at the most intrinsic level, where a sense of imperfection may be rooted. Whereas, many dysfunctional individuals may feel the need to spend endless hours with a therapist or priest, *practicing* grace in our lives works directly on healing psychological impairments. Acknowledging negative feelings is the first step; releasing them is the second; nurturing the healing is the final stage.

Through the ages, many theories have suggested various means for finding happiness. However, the reality is that only three key factors are required for reaching a true state of happiness, a sense of: (1) hope, (2) purpose and (3) balance in our lives. *The power of grace supports us by integrating these factors within our mind-set; it grounds positive thinking, a sense of service, as well as equilibrium within our lives, smoothing out the ripples caused by "egotism."*

Needless to say, mistakes can make us feel vulnerable. But it doesn't have to be that way. We don't have to obsess over what could have been, should have been or would have been. There is no need to waste time with mistakes: we simply vow to learn from them, moving forward. If we learn from our mistakes, they have served their purpose; and therefore, there is no need to continually rehash them. Mistakes are simply a means to success! And the sweet experiences are never as melodic without mistakes. In fact, pure positivity without checks and balances can wear us down, stretching our resources to the limit. Thus, so-called mistakes can enrich our lives with a greater sense of appreciation.

Every day, every moment, we make choices, whether we are conscious of the process or not. We can take *conscious* control of this process, shifting gears by means of our attitude. We can learn to value all things, for appreciation is grace! This attitude moves us beyond the entrapment of obsession. As we progress in consciousness, appreciation becomes our normal state of mind. It is about rediscovering the childlike qualities we lose in adulthood. This requires that we open our hearts and keep our egos flexible. It is also about shifting our focus from ego to Higher Self. We have the power to choose how to react to circumstances. Whether we feel appreciative or hateful, it is a choice that we alone make. That is our power — to choose how we feel, for no one can choose for us.

The ability to choose our focus should not be underestimated for the power that it is. Beliefs mold reality: they are like seeds that sprout and change the direction of our lives. As we gradually recalibrate our attitude — our mind-set — we also retune our personal frequency. Each of us has a specific, unique frequency; it is our personalized electro-magnetic signature. And without investing effort, patience and grace in our personal frequency, we become dependent on the mercy of external circumstances.

•**Laughter.** Another means for programming grace into our mind-set is the simple act of laughter. It is a powerful process that releases stress and integrates appreciation within our lives. When we laugh, we lighten the mood and relax our attitude. Some shamans even suggest that laughter is a divine trait. Certainly, at the very least, it is a childlike characteristic. Observations prove that children tend to laugh more than adults; and their laughter tends to be based on simpler, more innocent actions. Furthermore, they tend to tickle each other, whereas adults rarely do. Tickling, as an initiator of laughter, has two interesting qualities: we cannot tickle ourselves into laughing, and we tend not to tickle strangers. So it appears that tickling is a social act for bonding. How often do you see adults tickling each other? With adults, tickling tends to level off around the age of 40. It appears to be an act rejected by the ego, due to its hardened outlook on Life. The harsh reality of Life tends to make the ego progressively more brittle. This may be the reason older individuals tend to laugh more at painful situations endured by others, whether they be "harmless" accidents or deadly misfortunes.

The phrase "laugh and the world laughs with you" suggests that laughter is contagious. When we hear others laugh, we tend to react with laughter of our own, becoming part of a chain reaction. The role of laughter in psychotherapy has been debated for countless ages. There have always been those who uphold laughter's therapeutic benefits, while critics have disdainfully dismissed it as a simple instinctive reaction. Yet we do not need "experts" to convince us that laughter helps release stress, shifting our attitude into positive mode. This insight is, after all, common sense! Some thinkers have even suggested that laughter is a spiritual expression of the soul. When we laugh at humorous, innocent observations, the process appears to flow from the deepest part of our soul. Thus, when we come to a point in our lives when we are unable to perceive the humor of silly circumstances, it is because the ego has become hardened and has distanced itself from the Higher Self.

It is a matter of personal choice. We can grow old with a callused, cynical attitude. Or we can strive to maintain a flexible ego, expanding our personal boundaries into ever-wider views. We can make the smart choice to remain open to our childlike persona, always choosing grace over resentment. We can choose to perceive the humor within all things, because it helps us remain mentally, emotionally and spiritually balanced.

Needless to say, what amuses one individual may offend another. Although humor is a universal human trait, not all topics are humorous to all individuals nor to all cultures. Therefore, it is sometimes best to laugh only within ourselves. When sharing humor with others, it becomes a positive force only when there is common rapport. Learning to appreciate the lighter side of Life takes time; "practice makes perfect"! And while laughter can be spontaneous, we can still learn to entrain spontaneity into our consciousness. We encourage this process by simply remaining open to it.

Of course, humor can be risky; but it is better to try and learn in the process. The least riskiest humor is usually about ourselves. If we fear looking foolish to others, it is because our ego is insecure. When we are able to laugh at our selves, it is an indication that our self confidence is well grounded and that our ego's protective shell is flexible. Ask yourself: Do you prefer a life colored with dark cynicism? Or do you prefer a life eased with the light of humor? Without humor, Life is like a vehicle without suspension coils — every jolt is felt at its most severe level.

Comedians understand the power of humor in easing painful situations. In this respect, it is a tool for overcoming dark experiences. It is a weapon for winning the battle between light and darkness. When negative forces hit hard, we don't have to feel powerless. After taking a moment to recuperate, we can minimize painful experiences with humor, softening their impact. We can transcend our darkest experiences, lifting ourselves above despair. Thus laughter, appreciation and grace are security blankets that can insulate us from our fears and traumas.

Certainly, not all traumatic experiences are easily dismissed or overcome. They may include the death of a loved one, for example, and we must allow a period of grieving. Such expressions are simply part of the human equation. Humor, in such circumstances, may not be immediately appropriate.

•**Alternate tools**. The power of grace can also be enhanced through other means: (1) chanting, (2) music, and (3) meditation. These instruments are particularly appropriate for individuals with hardened egos. Although external methods are not strictly necessary for grace transformation, yet some egos are especially resistant to change. Instrumental factors are really distractions for the ego, which tends to require physical expression in order to relate to spiritual concepts. Physically structured programs are simply meant to appease the ego's desire for such activity. Logic, rationality and willpower are strategies the ego can relate to. Therefore, they can be integrated into systems involving music, chanting or meditation, which can help the ego reconstitute its flexibility.

Rhythmic energy is one of the most integral principles found throughout the universe. For example, the rhythm of beating drums can affect the heart with a frequency of ecstasy. There is some truth to the esoteric observation that, "at the heart of all forms of rhythm there is the divine, creative force," permeating and shaping reality. Thus this principle is integrated into the spiritual beliefs of many religions throughout the world. Not only does rhythm help focus consciousness, it can also help unify a group consciousness. This is not, however, a metaphysical principle available only to religions; it is something common to the human condition, a factor integrated within our brain's wiring.

Chanting is a manifestation of the rhythm principle. It can be a powerful force for personal growth, helping to instill a sense of peace within our hearts and minds. Rhythmic sounds can help bring our consciousness into a focused state in two ways: (1) by distracting the ego, and (2) by integrating our three minds through the perfect resonance of one intention. Because chanting is a conscious effort that creates a focused frequency, it can be a powerful means for bypassing the ego's analytical tendency and bridging it with the Higher Self.

Chanting is not necessarily about surrendering to our passions. Rather, it can be about harnessing and focusing our desires within one purpose. It can direct the flow of energy into a focused consciousness, thereby establishing a connection with our creative energy. It can connect the earthly ego with something much greater and wider than itself — our Divine Selves. Just as our feet often tap in rhythm with music, our consciousness will move to the rhythm of the universe. Sound vibrations affect not only our consciousness via the ears; they also enter through the skin and bones. This is why deaf musicians can still create music — because they perform by *feeling* sound vibrations.

In the scheme of universal physics, sound energy can lead to other types of energy — mechanical, heat, electro-magnetic or light, for example. Theoretically, sound waves are eternal, for their energy is continuous as they transform into other types of energy. Although a sound wave eventually becomes indiscernible, its energy simply transmutes into other forms of energy. So in a way, sound can be a bridge to other forms of energy. It can unify matter and energy; it can penetrate air, water and physical objects, pushing and shaping other forms of energy towards a specific frequency. The historical breaking of the walls of Jericho is an example of the ultimate power of sound.

More importantly, sound can be harnessed for instilling grace within our hearts and minds. The right resonance can also radiate a sense of grace unto other bodies, through the principle of sympathetic frequency. For example, when two pendulum clocks are set side by side, their pendulums eventually synchronize their swings into the exact same rhythm. The same principle applies to individuals in proximity.

Music, without doubt, has universal appeal among all cultures and individuals. It appears that humans are wired to appreciate music, though we all have individual preferences. Thus, it should not be surprising that Life is inherently musical, for the qualities of music — rhythm and mathematical beat — are found everywhere in Nature, from atoms, to cellular structure, to astronomical bodies. Grace itself has its own musical beat at the highest celestial dimension. Therefore music of our liking can be a powerful means for expressing common nirvana. In fact, certain fundamental tones and rhythms can uplift us into a state of grace, reminding us of our divine nature.

Music has the capacity to anchor specific associations within our minds and hearts. By triggering powerful feelings, it is able to initiate a shifting of consciousness, if only momentarily. As the body and mind beat as one, the heart and brain frequencies also become entrained to the melodic rhythm. In this manner, music can encourage bonding among team members. Healers can also harness the power of music, thereby improving quality of life. Of course, *how* we perceive and process music is as important as the quality of the music. And there is a difference between "hearing" and "listening." In other words, we must be receptive to music for it to manifest its power within our lives. With this objective in mind, music can focus body and consciousness accordingly. But although the mind craves rhythm, it also develops tolerance to specific rhythms. Thus variety is indeed "the spice of life!"

Meditation. While music can instill us with spiritual feelings, meditation can do the same. It can be a tool for entraining rhythm within the psyche. Regardless of its origins — religious, psychological or cultural — contemplative practices known as meditation combine chanting with focused consciousness with the intent of tuning into the divine. The power of meditation can be appreciated through understanding the phenomenon of resonance, which is "the re-sounding of vibration." This refers to the principle that everything — from subatomic particles to planets — resonates with specific frequencies. In fact, without resonance there would be no Life.

When we meditate with the intent of receiving grace, we simultaneously radiate this energy from our consciousness. The intent we hold is very important. If we focus on the grosser objectives of the ego, that will be our manifested reality. On the other hand, when we focus on spiritual concepts of divinity, it aligns the ego with our

Higher Selves. The "animal self" (the ego) can be encouraged to work in partnership with the "godly self" (the Superconscious). Meditative practices integrate rhythmic resonance with intent, thereby bridging the ego's need for expression with divine creativity. Thus they can be a vehicle for teaching the ego how to express a sense of grace.

Whatever the intent, it can be empowered to manifest accordingly. So meditation is a practical means for accomplishing definitive objectives. Although it is often packaged as a religious practice, it is really about expressing human needs. It is about expressing our divine heritage in the earthly realm. It is certainly not a supernatural practice; it is a supernormal one, for it is simply a structured, mental discipline — of ego and Superconscious cooperating in partnership. Meditation can also be structured in a ritualized format. In reality, ritual is quite an ordinary, human practice; we are all wired for ritual. For instance, we all carry out ritualized patterns on a daily basis — whether it be brushing our teeth, dressing for work, watching TV, or exercising in the gym. The key difference between mundane rituals versus spiritual ones is the objective.

The Magical Equation. Structured meditation is really a patterned equation created with tones, rhythms, pictures and emotions of our choosing. While chanting during meditation preoccupies the ego with physical activity, the chanted *mantrum* also serves as the template on which we engrave our intention. And when imbued with passionate energy, it colors and enlivens the intent. While sound frequencies do impress their energies on our objective, nevertheless the most important part of the meditated equation is the intent. Thus the intent to bless our lives with grace is energized by the mantrum and enlivened by our passion.

While the Higher Self has no need for ritualized meditation, the ego finds it quite satisfying: Not only does meditation focus the ego's attention; it also helps it relate to the concept of divine creation. The ego only understands *physical* creation — creating through physical force; whereas the Higher Self creates *divinely* —

through direct manipulation of energy. Thus by means of meditation, life can become more fluid; it can flow more "naturally" with successful expression. It also allows the ego to fulfill its part as a channel for the Higher Self's expression.

The connection between meditation and grace is beautifully exemplified by the Serenity Prayer:

Grant me the serenity to accept
the things I cannot change,
Courage to change the things I can,
and the wisdom to know the difference.

By every definition, this prayer is a powerful equation; it incorporates three key factors: 1) a mantrum to distract the ego, 2) the intent to receive acceptance, courage and wisdom, and 3) a written format which allows persistent application. This prayer can enhance grace in our lives, because its first objective is to help us *accept* the things we cannot change. But acceptance is tempered with the *intent* to manifest serenity, courage and wisdom in our lives as well — factors that are naturally rendered by grace.

Most everyone who reaches a sense of success does so because *structure, visualization and persistence* have been key factors in their personal equation. The difference is that meditation incorporates these factors within a formalized system. And when we implement it for the expression of grace, its power is radiated many times over. If we doubt the power of meditation to improve our lives, the proof is in the experience. We simply have to practice meditation and observe the results to fully appreciate its value.

140

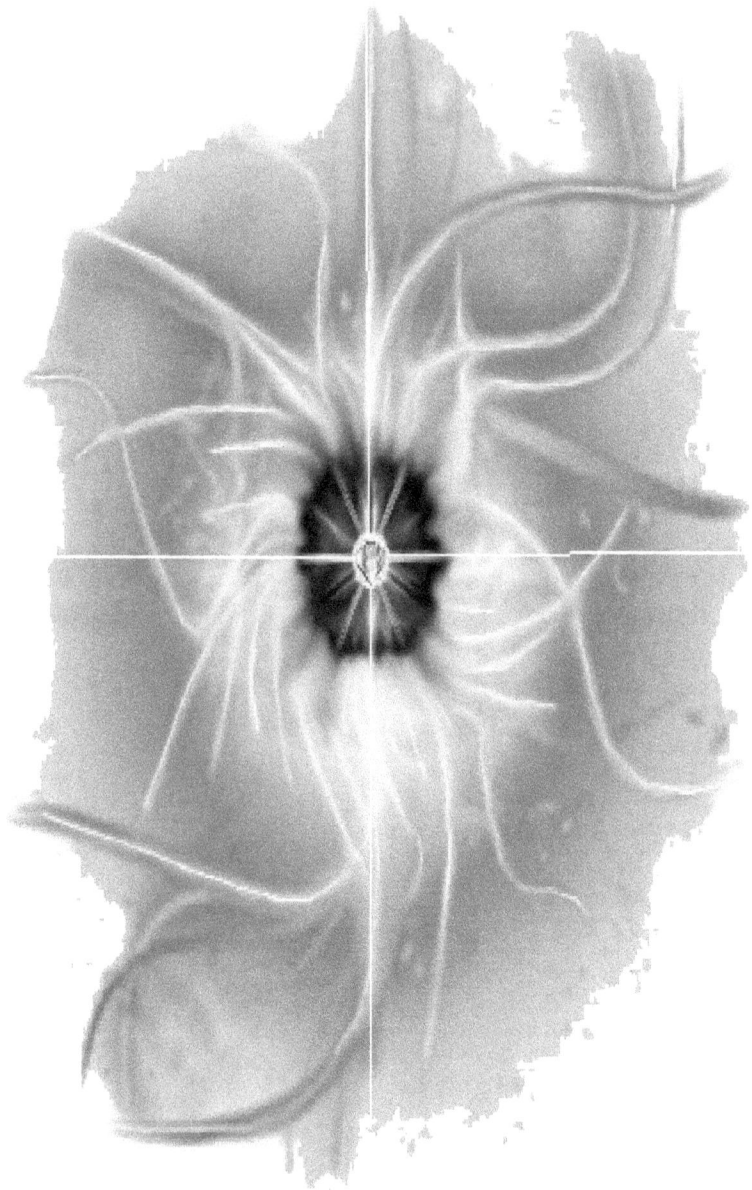

CHAPTER SEVEN

LET IT SHINE

There are many ways to describe the power of grace because — like a multi-faceted diamond — it reflects brilliance from many angles. In simplest terms, it can be understood as compassion, reverence and inclusiveness. Essentially, this means respecting all aspects of Life, because everything has its purpose and place in the bigger scheme of things. It means showing respect to our fellow humans, whether we like them or not. It means respecting Mother Earth, whether we understand how she supports us or not. Regardless of what the things or people are, they are honored simply for being.

There are esoteric descriptions of grace as well. For example, some thinkers have speculated that grace manifests as the Holy Spirit. And still others have theorized that grace can be mathematically expressed, since everything can be defined in mathematical terms. Even now, as physicists continue their search for the *Theory of Everything* — a mathematical equation tying all realities into one simple expression — there is universal concurrence that mathematics is the foundation of reality. In relation to this, it is important to grasp that *everything* is about energy at the most intrinsic level. Life *is* energy! And since energy can be quantified and measured, every bit of energy can be expressed mathematically. Thus all things — including grace — can be codified as mathematical equations.

The whole of reality has sometimes been described as a vast computer program, one which continually processes information at an ever compounding rate. In this manner, it is perpetually expanding what we know as "reality." From atoms to people, information and mathematics are an integral part of the fabric of reality. *Everything* is imbued with mathematics, geometry and pattern, whether we perceive it or not. And since the whole universe is ordered by means of numbers, it is only logical that it would be maintained harmoniously in mathematical terms as well. In this regard, the force of grace is the principle that moves things back into equilibrium. Its function is similar to a software algorithm: it is created expressly for solving unforeseen problems. If the whole of Life is one comprehensive software program, is it not logical that it would include an algorithm for self correction? Otherwise, an accumulation of errors would eventually lead to dangerous states of imbalance.

In spiritual terms, grace has been described as the Great Equalizer, for its sole purpose is to smooth out the bumps, kinks and so-called errors in Life — always bringing reality back into a balanced state. Even within our personal lives, some kind of force is needed to balance things out. This is Divine Grace.

Historically speaking, karma (or sin) has been the predominant equalizer within humanity. During our initial stage of development as a species, karma and sin have been the primary means by which we have learned about Life. Essentially, it has been about learning to work with the Principle of Cause and Effect - e.g., "an eye for an eye."

Humanity has now reached a point where it is ready to move to the next level of understanding, where grace plays a dominant role in our spiritual growth. Eventually and gradually, the legalism now predominant in our thinking will be replaced with the gentler force of grace, where everyone will be supported by the light of grace. Gone will be the punitive laws of karma and the curse of accumulated sin.

Although humanity's origins are divine, we are still subject to universal principles. (see book 4) Thus living within a state of grace does not mean that we are free to break universal principles without consequences. There is much confusion and misunderstanding in that regard, especially among those who resist the concept of grace. The purpose, power and potential of grace has been deliberately scrambled by controlling egos (and dark mentalities). So there is a real need to analyze, describe and share the true nature of Divine Grace.

Ever since the Great Healer introduced the concept to the world, forces of darkness have counter attacked by confusing the issue. What these "dark forces" may be has been debated throughout the centuries. (see book 4) But the bottom line is that forces working to promote confusion, ignorance and fear have encouraged the human ego to view grace with hostility. Yet we can't place full blame on external "forces." Ultimately, we have only our frail egos to blame.

For too long, the true origin of humanity has been

muddled with convoluted, contradictory beliefs. For example, religious dogma often teaches that we are children of God — yet it also teaches that we are unworthy of respect due to our sins or bad karma. That is the ego's take: demanding that everyone *earn* his or her passage up the hierarchical ladder of respect. But the Higher Self says "no!" to this approach, reminding us that we are divine by nature. As children of God, we are worthy of Divine Grace — no exceptions, no excuses! Do we really have to perform mundane sacrifices to become worthy? There is nothing to earn; nothing to prove. We only have to readjust our hearts.

As an imperfect, mirror image of our Higher Selves, the ego is geared for physical survival. So spiritual insights initially appear impractical, alien and even ridiculous to the earthbound ego. Fortunately, it does have the capacity to learn the importance and practicality of grace. However, a leap of faith is required before it can do so, before it can fully partner with the Higher Self.

From the ego's simplistic point of view, grace seems to tempt us to push beyond limits of acceptable behavior. After all, to the ego, humans are wild creatures, easily corrupted and readily induced into barbarism. So they must be controlled with a combination of religious dogma and civil laws. Institutions are the ego's solution for controlling our animal nature — for it is leery of its destructive capabilities. The ego imagines that everyone would abuse the "loopholes" that Divine Grace appears to offer. Surely, the world would go mad with chaos! But in fact, the opposite is true: there are no loopholes! The ego is sorely mistaken in believing that grace leads to disorderly conduct and more evil. Thus, because it cannot initially grasp the full positive implications of this "alien" concept, the ego has to take a leap of faith. Only then is there integration of our mirror selves, which leads to a more successful expression of our full consciousness.

Our Higher Selves project the understanding that "our best" is *always* good enough, for it has patience, understanding and gratitude for our circumstances. There is never judgement. From the divine perspective, the journey is just as important as the destination. The goal, of course, is full integration of our consciousness, which develops as we discover, embrace and practice spiritual insights. On the other hand, we must also *unlearn* convoluted concepts that have been adopted along the way. Some of these misconceptions have misrepresented our true nature; others have simply confused the true nature of reality.

Integrity and fairness are integral parts of the grace equation. Practicing graciousness in our own lives means encouraging others to appreciate the gifts of Life. It means saying "yes" to Life; it means saying "yes" to building bridges rather than barriers. And it is certainly about allowing others the freedom to learn from their own mistakes, for grace and freedom are inclusive of each other; one cannot be expressed without the other.

Every turn in our lives is an opportunity to build a better future; every challenge an opportunity to express our divine essence. Although the ego grows weary of problems, it is the only way it learns. Imagine a reality without problems or disagreements. Would there be effort to evolve in understanding? Only effort brings about progress; challenge promotes growth. That is why the ego is important to the Higher Self: for the role it plays in bringing challenge into our consciousness.

The Higher Self never judges anyone as immoral, sinful or inferior, for the very nature of grace disallows conditional expression. Everyone and everything is worthy of grace — no ifs, buts or whys! From its perspective, everyone is an expression of divinity; thus everyone must be encouraged to follow their bliss.

As concepts of sin and karma are gradually diminished from our consciousness, Earth will be transformed into a planet of grace — for that is its destiny. As more and more individuals throw off their mental shackles, the power of grace will reach a critical mass, where it becomes the norm. Humans will no longer be perceived as "sinners" but as the divine souls they truly are.

As grace becomes an integral part of our consciousness, divine attributes within our DNA will manifest as well, having been triggered by the grace frequency. These genetic codes will unfold latent powers that have been dormant for millennia. Centuries ago, the Great Healer declared that humanity would eventually develop the power to "move mountains." And while "absolute power absolutely corrupts," grace tempers this potential corruption. Thus, our birthright as co-creators will manifest fully as the ego is firmly anchored within our divine consciousness.

BIBLIOGRAPHY
& RECOMMENDED READING

Aronson, B.C. *Grace.* 2006

Byrne, Rhonda. *The Magic.* 2012

Campbell, David C. *The Children of Grace*. 2011

Campbell, Don. *The Mozart Effect.* 2001

Diener & Biswas-Diener. *Happiness.* 2008

Dwoskin, Hale. *The Sedona Method.* 2007

Gass, Robert. *Chanting.* 1999

Klein, Allen. *The Healing Power of Humor.* 1989

Lama, Dalai. *Many Ways to Nirvana.* 2004

Lyubomirsky, Sonja. *The How of Happiness.* 2007

Peirce, Penney. *Frequency.* 2009

Van Auken, John. *From Karma To Grace*. 2010

Wilde, Stuart. *Grace, Gaia, and the End of Days.* 2009

Yancey, Philip. *What's So Amazing About Grace?* 1997

154

www.ingramcontent.com/pod-product-compliance
Lightning Source LLC
LaVergne TN
LVHW011239080426
835509LV00005B/548